EPISTLES OF JOHN & JUDE
A SELF-STUDY GUIDE

Irving L. Jensen

MOODY PRESS
CHICAGO

©1971 by
THE MOODY BIBLE INSTITUTE
OF CHICAGO

Scripture quotations, unless noted otherwise, are taken from the King James Version.

ISBN: 0-8024-4461-X

2 3 4 5 6 7 Printing/EP/Year 01 00 99 98 97 96

Printed in the United States of America

Contents

Introduction

The world today is at a low ebb spiritually. The teeming masses are without God and without hope. And when we measure the pulse of the Christian church today, we are alarmed—if we are honest. Laodicean apostasy is becoming more and more prevalent, rebuked anew by the Lord's word of Revelation 3:17: "Thou sayest, I am rich, and increased with goods, and have need of nothing; and knowest not that thou are wretched, and miserable, and poor, and blind, and naked."

Christians who are alert to the alarming trends in the church today need to beware lest they panic and flee, throw up their hands, and cast away their weapons. God wants His children always to remember that there is no darkness so black that His light cannot pierce it; that Satan is not so strong that God's Son cannot defeat him; that the believer is not so weak that God's Spirit cannot empower him. These are some of the reasons for God's including in the New Testament the epistles of John and Jude. One might generalize the content of these epistles by saying that they teach:

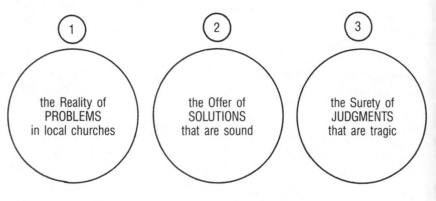

1	2	3
the Reality of PROBLEMS in local churches	the Offer of SOLUTIONS that are sound	the Surety of JUDGMENTS that are tragic

So if we are alarmed over the state and condition of our churches and the world, let us study these epistles to see what God says and how He wants to use us in the circumstances.

- *Suggestions for Study:*

The author has given various suggestions for individual and group Bible study in the other manuals of this study series. The one bit of advice that he feels can never be overstated is this: see exactly what the Bible says (LOOK); and record on paper what you see (JOT IT DOWN!). Spend much time with the Bible text itself, so that you can arrive at sound interpretations and make necessary applications. Follow the directions of each lesson faithfully, and you will find yourself digging in the Bible text continually. Practical suggestions for Bible study are treated at length in the author's book *Independent Bible Study.*

When used for Bible study groups, each lesson need not be completed in one group session. Some lessons, because of length, are better studied in two or more units. The leader of your group should determine the length of each study unit.

There are hindrances to profitable Bible study, which everyone should beware. Think about each of these listed below, and work on dispelling those that hinder you personally:

> disinterest
> delay
> difficulty
> distraction
> distress
> digression

The heart attitude of *expectancy* is a must for getting the most out of Bible study. As you begin to study the epistles discussed in this manual, desire the experience reflected by this testimony:

Did not our hearts
 GLOW WITHIN US
  while He
  was talking to us on the road and
  OPENED THE SCRIPTURES to us? (Luke 24:32, *Berkeley*).

Lesson 1
The Man John

Although John's biographical data is understandably fragmentary, we have enough information for a portrait. As you proceed with this lesson, be sure to read each reference cited for whatever information it gives concerning the man John, the beloved disciple of Jesus. Consider your study of this lesson to be a vital introduction to your study of the text of the epistles in the later lessons. For to be acquainted with the man John is to stand in his shoes, as it were, and empathize with him as he shares the truths so precious and glorious in *his* sight.

I. NAME

The name John was a common one in Jesus' day, just as it was in Old Testament days and as it is today. The Greek name is *Ioannes*, derived from the Hebrew *Yohanan*, which means literally "Jehovah is gracious." Often this name was given to a child as a testimony of the parents' gratitude to God for the gift of a baby (cf. 1 Chron. 3:15).

Five different men in the New Testament bear the name of John:

1. John the Baptist (e.g., Luke 1:57-66; Matt. 3:1)
2. John Mark (e.g., Acts 12:12; 2 Tim. 4:11)
3. Jona, or Jonas, father of Simon Peter (John 1:42; 21:15, 17)
4. John, a relative of Annas the high priest (Acts 4:6)
5. John son of Zebedee (Matt. 4:21), an apostle of Jesus (Matt. 10:2), who called himself "the elder" in 2 John 1 and 3 John 1. This John was the author of the epistles.

II. BIRTH

The place of John's birth may have been the city of Bethsaida, at the northern tip of the Sea of Galilee. This was the hometown of Philip, Andrew, and Peter (John 1:44). We do not know the date of his birth, but he may have been at least five years younger than Jesus.

III. FAMILY

John's mother was Salome (cf. Matt. 27:56 with Mark 15:40; 16:1). If, as suggested by John 19:25, Salome was a sister of Mary the mother of Jesus, then Jesus and John were cousins. This would partly explain the special place John had in Jesus' "inner circle."

John's father was Zebedee (Matt. 4:21; Mark 1:19), a fisherman on the Sea of Galilee. John had at least one brother, James the apostle (Matt. 4:21), who was executed by Herod Agrippa I around A.D. 44 (Acts 12:1-2). Jesus surnamed both brothers Boanerges, or "sons of thunder," a name indicating perhaps a fiery personality in the young men (cf. Luke 9:52-56). Before becoming a disciple of Jesus, John was in the fishing trade with his father and brother.

It appears that John's parents were well to do, as suggested by the following:

1. Their household had servants (Mark 1:20).
2. Salome helped with the financial support of Jesus during His public ministry (Luke 8:3; Mark 15:40-41).
3. Salome bought spices for Jesus' body (Mark 16:1).
4. John was a personal acquaintance of the high priest (John 18:15), and usually high priests were of the upper class.

IV. EDUCATION

John as a boy and youth very likely had a thorough Jewish religious training at home. Devout Jewish parents, such as Salome was, placed a priority on this. The reference of Acts 4:13 to Peter and John's being "unlearned and ignorant men" simply tells us that these apostles did not have *formal* training in the rabbinical schools of that day. In present-day parlance, they were well-informed Christian laymen without a theology degree. As a disciple of John the Baptist (cf. John 1:35), John must have learned much from the forerunner of Jesus.

V. EXPERIENCE

John's life may be divided into two eras: (1) before meeting Jesus, and (2) after meeting Jesus. Of that first era we know practically nothing. The second era was of two periods, which we shall identify as (1) pre-Pentecost period (i.e., up to the event of Acts 2) and (2) post-Pentecost period. Let us now study each of these periods, keeping in mind that the John who, toward the end of his life, wrote the epistles of our study, is the John who was molded and perfected by the experiences of the periods.

A. Pre-Pentecost Period

The approximate three and a half years of Jesus' public ministry constituted this pre-Pentecost period. John was with Jesus most of this time. He was the disciple greatly loved by the Master (read John 21:7, 20). Of the three disciples of Jesus' "inner circle" (Peter, James, and John), John was the most prominent, whereas Peter was the most active one. (Read Mark. 5:37; Matt. 17:1; 26:37.)

Stages of discipleship. The part John played in Jesus' public ministry may be broken down according to three stages. (Read all the passages cited.)

1. First Stage (during the first year of Jesus' ministry)
   a. John meets Jesus and becomes one of His disciples (John 1:35-39).
   b. John is with Jesus during most of the first year of Jesus' public ministry.
   c. John returns to the fishing occupation, at least temporarily. (We cannot be sure of this transfer of activity.)

2. Second Stage (at the beginning of the second year of Jesus' ministry)
   a. Jesus calls disciples (Peter and Andrew; James and John) to become "fishers of men" (Matt. 4:18-22; Mark 1:16-20; Luke 5:1-11).
   b. Jesus continues His training of the disciples to be witnesses for Him.

3. Third Stage (four months into the second year of Jesus' public ministry)

8

a. John with eleven others is ordained to the apostolate (Matt. 10:2-4; Mark 3:13-19; Luke 6:12-19). What three aspects of this ordination are mentioned in Mark 3:14-15?

_____

_____

_____

b. John remains close to Jesus up to His Gethsemane experience (read Matt. 26:37ff.), then flees from His presence at His arrest (Matt. 26:56).

c. John is one of the first ones to view the empty sepulcher of Jesus (John 20:1-10).

d. John with the other apostles obeys Jesus' command to wait in Jerusalem for the descent of the Holy Spirit upon them (Acts 1:8, 12-14).

Key Experiences. There were many key experiences of John as he served his Master during this pre-Pentecost period. On page 7 are listed the references to most of these. Read each passage, and record the experience and its significance for John. (Consider also the surrounding context in each case.)

B. Post-Pentecost Period

From Galatians 2:9 we learn that Peter (Cephas), James, and John were leaders of the church at Jerusalem during the first years after Pentecost. Read these passages, which record some of John's activities during this time: Acts 3:1ff.; 4:1-22; 8:14-15. After chapter 8 of Acts there is no mention of John, though he surely attended the Jerusalem Council of Acts 15 *if* he was in the vicinity at the time. There is no mention of him in Acts 21, when Paul was in Jerusalem, which would point to the fact that probably by this time at least John had moved to another place.

The latter years of John's life were probably spent around Ephesus, hub city of Asia Minor, where the apostle was teaching, preaching, and writing. The Bible books he wrote (the gospel, three epistles, Revelation) were all probably written between A.D. 85 and 96. Ephesus, you may recall, was the city where Paul spent about three years on his third missionary journey, evangelizing and teaching the Word of God to many converts (Acts 19:1-20). How strong and spiritually mature the young Ephesian church became is suggested by Acts 19:20 and by the profound depths of Paul's epistle to the Ephesians, which the apostle wrote from prison at Rome. It was among such Ephesian Christians that John ministered during the last years of his life.

Passage	Experience	Significance
Mark 5:37; Luke 8:51		
Matthew 17:1; Mark 9:2; Luke 9:28		
Mark 9:38; Luke 9:49		
Luke 9:54		
Mark 10:35		
Mark 13:3		
Luke 22:8		
John 13:23, 25		
Matthew 26:37; Mark 14:33, 37		
Matthew 26:56		
John 18:15-16		
John 19:26		
John 20:2-3		
John 21:1-7		
John 21:20-24		

Although John's home may have been in Ephesus at this time, he was well acquainted with churches in surrounding cities, such as Smyrna, Pergamos, Thyatira, Sardis, Philadelphia, and Laodicea. (Consult a map for these locations.) These are the churches to whom he sent the scroll of his visions received on the island of Patmos, around A.D. 95 (Rev. 1:9-11).

VI. DEATH

John apparently died in Ephesus soon after writing Revelation. His age at death was about 100. Read John 21:23, and note an interesting reference to the apostle made by Jesus. Of this, *Unger's Bible Dictionary* comments:

> If to this [known lot of John, including the Patmos experience] we add that he must have outlived all, or nearly all, of those who had been the friends and companions even of his maturer years; that this lingering age gave strength to an old impression that his Lord had promised him immortality (John 21:23); that, as if remembering the actual words which had been thus perverted, the longing of his soul gathered itself up in the cry, "Even so, come, Lord Jesus" (Rev. 22:20), we have stated all that has any claim to the character of historical truth.[1]

We are admitting to sincere curiosity when we say we would like to know how soon after writing, "Even so, come, Lord Jesus," (Rev. 22:20) John's spirit was ushered into the presence of Christ.

VII. CHARACTER

John, like Peter, is an example of a man with an intense, vigorous nature, which Christ directed to the glory of God. At times John's intensity was unfortunately the channel for evil words and deeds. Read Mark 9:38; Luke 9:49, 54; Matthew 20:20-28; Mark 10:35, and observe John in the dark moments of intolerance, vindictiveness, undue vehemence, and selfish ambition. For the most part, however, the New Testament's picture of John is an attractive and beautiful one. Charles C. Ryrie says, "In actions, in love for the brethren, in condemnation of heresy, John was the intense apostle."[2] Whereas Paul is known as the apostle of faith, and Peter the apostle of hope, John is referred to as the apostle of love. Writes Tenney, "As Christ tamed his ardor and purified it of unrestrained

---

1. Merrill F. Unger, *Unger's Bible Dictionary* (Chicago: Moody, 1957), p. 597.
2. Charles C. Ryrie, "I, II, III John," in *The Wycliffe Bible Commentary*, p. 1463.

violence, John became the apostle of love whose devotion was not excelled by that of any other writer of the New Testment."[3] His tender concern for other Christians is manifested most clearly in his epistles, where he addresses his readers as "my little children" and "beloved." As we study John's epistles we will be learning more of the character of the one so loved of Christ.

SOME REVIEW QUESTIONS

See how many of the following you can complete without referring back to the lesson.

1. What does the Hebrew word for John mean, literally?

2. Who are the different Johns of the New Testament?

3. Describe what is known of John's family.

4. Reconstruct a probable biography of John up to his meeting Jesus for the first time. How did he compare in age with Jesus?

5. Review the three stages of John's ministry in his association with Jesus.

6. Why do you think Jesus chose John to be one of His closest disciples?

7. What was John's ministry after Pentecost while he remained in Jerusalem?

8. What was John's ministry at Ephesus up to the time of his death?

9. What Bible books did John write, and when did he write them?

10. Write a paragraph describing the character of John. If you are studying in a group, you may want to discuss this subject.

---

3. Merrill C. Tenney, *New Testament Survey*, rev. ed. (Grand Rapids: Eerdmans, 1961), p. 189.

Lesson 2
Background and Survey of 1 John

God included in the New Testament a few books written at least fifty years after Jesus' ascension in about A.D. 33. Most of the New Testament books were written earlier, from about A.D. 45 to the years just prior to the fall of Jerusalem (A.D. 70). These latter books were written to verbalize the authoritative basis of the Christian church, and to give God's answers to man's questions about the historical facts of Jesus' life and about interpretations and significances of those facts. The five books (a gospel, three epistles, Revelation) written at the end of the century (about A.D. 85 to A.D. 96) were written by the same man—the apostle John. Besides his unique old-age experience of visions on the isle of Patmos (when he wrote the book of Revelation), John had the privilege of meditating long on the wonderful truths of Jesus' life. He recorded his reflections under the inspiration of the Holy Spirit in a gospel record and in three epistles. The longest of the three epistles, 1 John, is the book we will study first in this manual.

Chart A shows a possible chronological order of the writing of the twenty-seven New Testament books.[1] From it you can learn something of the setting of John's epistles. Observe the event of the fall of Jerusalem, and note how many years had elapsed between the writings of Peter and of John. As you think about these and other things, arrive at some *possible* answers to the following questions:

---

1. The dates of most of the books are fairly dependable, plus or minus a couple of years in some cases. The dates of the writing of a few books, such as Mark, are the least sure because of sparse data.

CHRONOLOGICAL PUBLISHING DATES
OF THE NEW TESTAMENT BOOKS

BOOK	AUTHOR	PLACE WRITTEN	DATE A.D.	PERIODS		
				Personnel	Apostolic Literature	Church
James	– James	Jerusalem	45			
Galatians			48			
1 Thessalonians		Corinth	52	FIRST		
2 Thessalonians	– Paul			PAULINE		
1 Corinthians		Ephesus	55	PERIOD	BEGINNINGS —about 15 years	FOUNDING
2 Corinthians		Macedonia				
Romans		Corinth	56			
Matthew	– Matthew	Jerusalem?		FIRST		
Luke	– Luke	Rome	61	HISTORICAL		
Acts				RECORDS		
Colossians				CENTRAL		
Ephesians				PAULINE		
Philemon	Paul	Rome	61	PERIOD		
Philippians						
1 Timothy			62			
Titus	– Paul	Rome		PAUL'S		
2 Timothy			67	LEGACY	CENTRAL —about 10 years	ESTABLISHING
Hebrews	– ?					
Jude	– Jude					
1 Peter						
2 Peter	– Peter		68?	PETER'S		
Mark	– Mark			LEGACY		
FALL OF JERUSALEM A.D. 70					15 "silent" years	
John		Ephesus?	85			
1 John						
2 John	– John			JOHN'S	CLOSING —about 10 years	CONTINUING
3 John				LEGACY		
Revelation		Patmos	96			

1. Why did God inspire John's books to be written so long after the other books of the New Testament?

_____

_____

2. What emphases might you expect to see in books written at this time? Why?

_____

_____

Throughout the centuries there have been those who have seen in John's epistles only a mild, diluted version of the Christian message. J.P. Lange quotes one commentator as saying that John's first epistle lacks the freshness of direct life, that it is written in a tone "childishly effeminate."[2] Lange's reaction is that such a reproach "may be met by Hilgenfeld's declaration that this Epistle is one of the *most beautiful* writings of the New Testament, that it is peculiarly rich and original with reference to the subjective, intensive life of Christianity, and that the fresh, living, and attractive character of the Epistle consists just in the marked preference with which it introduces us into the inward experience of the true Christian life."[3]

D. Edmond Hiebert has written this excellent description of John's first epistle:

> The forcible simplicity of its sentences, the note of finality behind its utterances, the marvelous blending of gentle love and deep-cutting sternness of its contents, and the majesty of its ungarnished thoughts, have made 1 John a favorite with Christians everywhere. The simplicity of its language makes it intelligible to the simplest saint, while the profundity of its truths challenges the most accomplished scholar. Its grand theological revelations and its unwavering ethical demands have left their enduring impact upon the thought and life of the Christian Church.[4]

As you begin your study of these epistles, it is important that you have an attitude of expectancy as to how much the Holy Spirit

2. John Peter Lange, *Commentary on the Holy Scriptures; The First Epistle General of John* (Grand Rapids: Zondervan, n.d.) p. 6.
3. Ibid.
4. D. Edmond Hiebert, *An Introduction to the Non-Pauline Epistles*, p. 189. (This volume by Hiebert is recommended very highly as a help in one's study of the general epistles.)

15

will teach you. The epistles of John were not afterthoughts of God, a P.S. to His gospels and other epistles. They are part of God's *last* written words. Who does not give undivided attention to the last words of a man, as he approaches the end of his life? All the more should we be attentive to the words of the everliving God as we come to the closing chapters of His Book, the Bible.

I. BACKGROUND OF 1 JOHN

A. Author

Internal evidence and early church tradition give ample support to the view that the apostle John wrote the epistles as well as the fourth gospel.[5] Arguments favoring another author, such as a different John with the designation "John the elder," are not as strong.

Identification of the author of the fourth gospel is narrowed down to the one man John the apostle when one considers the following descriptions of the author (Note: Study this section not only for the identification of authorship but also to learn more about John, the person):

1. He was a Palestinian Jew. This is shown, for example, by his use of the Old Testament (John 6:45; 13:18; 19:37); by his knowledge of Jewish traditions (1:19-49; 2:6, 13; 3:25; 4:25; 5:1; 6:14-15; 7:26ff.; 10:22; 11:55; 12:13; 13:1; 18:28; 19:31, 42); and by his knowledge of Palestine (1:44, 46; 2:1; 4:47; 5:2; 9:7; 10:23; 11:54).

2. He was an eyewitness. This is shown by the exactness of details in his reporting (e.g., 1:29, 35, 43; 2:6; 4:40, 43; 5:5; 12:1, 6, 12; 13:26; 19:14, 20, 23, 34, 39; 20:7; 21:6); and by the intimate character descriptions that he gives of such men as Andrew, Philip, Thomas, Nathanael, and Nicodemus.

3. He was one of Jesus' intimate associates, the "beloved disciple." (See 13:23; 18:15-16; 19:26-27). Of these associates, James was killed in the early years of the church's life (Acts 12:2); and Peter, Thomas, and Philip are referred to in the gospel in the third person so frequently that they may be eliminated as possible authors. This leaves John son of Zebedee as the most likely author of the gospel.

The next question is, Did the author of the fourth gospel also write 1 John? Most scholars agree that both books were written by the same man. Internal evidence, based mainly on similarities be-

---

5. Testimony is by such church Fathers as Polycrap, Irenaeus, Clement of Alexandria, and Tertullian.

tween the books, answers yes to the question. This evidence includes:

1. Similarities in the openings of each book (compare John 1:1-18 and 1 John 1:1-4)
2. Common phrases in the two books—for example, "only begotten" (John 1:14, 18; 3:16, 18; 1 Jn. 4:9; cf. 5:1, 18) and "born of God" (e.g., John 1:13; 1 John 3:9; 4:7; 5:1, 4, 18)
3. Similar grammatical and stylistic structure
4. Common themes prominent in both books—for example, love, light, life, abide, darkness, world, eternal life, new commandment, the Word, beginning, believe (98 times in the gospel, 9 times in the epistle), witness (33 times in the gospel, 6 times in the epistle)
5. Evidence in both books that the author personally knew Jesus (for 1 John, read 1:1-4 and 4:14)

When external evidence (such as testimony of the early church Fathers) is added to this strong internal evidence, the firm conclusion is reached that it was the apostle John who wrote the epistle as well as the gospel.

B. Date and Place of Writing

Although John's epistles do not identify where they were written, it is generally believed that the apostle wrote them from Ephesus. This conclusion is based on the concurrence of two data: (1) the epistles were written in the latter years of John's life; and (2) he spent his latter years in Ephesus.

The date of the writing of 1 John is approximately A.D. 85-90. The time is narrowed down to these years thus:

1. The epistle was written before the persecution of A.D. 95 under Emperor Domitian (otherwise the epistle might have made mention of this).
2. The epistle was written near the end of the century. Tenney suggests these hints: (a) the church and synagogue had become separate, (b) the controversy over faith vs. works had largely died out, (c) philosophical inquiries into the nature of Christ had begun.[6]

Of his five books, John wrote Revelation last (ca. A.D. 95). The gospel and 1 John were published about the same time. The logical relationship between the gospel and the epistle favors the former's being written first:

6. Merrill C. Tenney, *New Testament Survey*, p. 376.

17

Gospel	1 John
written to arouse faith (John 20:31)	written to establish certainty regarding that faith (1 John 5:13)
the good news historically	the good news experientially

C. Addressee

The readers of 1 John were probably a congregation or group of congregations of Asia Minor closely associated with the apostle. Read 2:7, 18, 20, 21, 24, 27; 3:11 for suggestions that the readers had been believers for a long time. Various teachers and preachers had ministered to the people living in the vicinity of Ephesus long before John wrote his books. (Among these were Paul, Acts 18:19; 19:1-20; Aquila and Priscilla, Acts 18:19, 24-26; Trophimus, Acts 21:29; the family of Onesiphorus, 2 Tim. 1:16-18; 4:19; and Timothy, 1 Tim. 1:3.) That most of John's readers were converts from paganism is only intimated by the absence of Old Testament quotations and by the warning regarding idols in the last sentence of the epistle (5:21).

Whoever the readers were, John knew them intimately. Hence the very personal, warm atmosphere of this letter to his "children."

D. Occasion and Purpose

John wrote this letter to Christians who were falling prey to the deceptive devices of Satan so common in our own day. Christians were fighting each other, and John was frank to declare that "he that hateth his brother is in darkness . . . and knoweth not whither he goeth, because that darkness hath blinded his eyes" (2:11). Christians were beginning to love the evil things of the world, and John wanted to warn them of the tragic consequencs. And then there were the false teachers—John calls them antichrists—who were trying to seduce the believers by false doctrine to draw them away from Christ. John warned his readers about such false teachers, encouraging them to stand true to the gospel and to abide in Christ. And then there were those who were doubting their own salvation. So John wrote to instill confidence, that such doubters might *know* that they had eternal life (5:13). In his gospel his purpose was to arouse a saving faith (John 20:31); in 1 John his purpose was to establish certainty regarding that faith.

The false teaching that John was especially trying to combat in his epistle was a form of Gnosticism in its infant stage. The basic tenet of the Gnostics was that matter was evil and spirit was good. One of the heresies that grew from this came to be known as Docetism, which held that Jesus did not have a real body (for then God would be identified with evil matter, or flesh), but that He *seemed* (Greek *dokeo*) to people to have a body. John made clear in his epistle that Jesus, the Son of God, appeared to man in real, human flesh. Read 1:1 and 4:2-3, and observe how unequivocally John declares this truth about Christ.

Four times in the epistle John specifically tells why he is writing this epistle. Read these verses, and record John's purposes:

1:4

_____

2:1

_____

2:26

_____

5:13

_____

E. Form and Style

1. *Form.* The first epistle of John has a unique combination of qualities as to form and style. It is classified as an epistle, even though it does not have the usual opening salutation, personal conclusion, references to proper names (except that of Jesus), or specific references to details of the lives of either the readers or the writer. Its many personal references to *writing* (e.g., "My little children, these things write I unto you, that ye sin not," 2:1a) are enough justification for considering the book as an epistle. On the basis of its contents one may say that the book is a personal letter of an aged Christian leader to a congregation of mature Christians with whom the writer was acquainted.

More will be said about the form, or structure, of the epistle in the Survey section of this lesson.

2. *Style.* In Hebraistic style, John writes short, simple, straightforward, picturesque sentences. The extended opening sentence

19

(1:1-3) is the one exception to the short pattern. Parallelisms and contrasts abound in the book. Concerning the latter, one writer comments, "His colours are black and white; there is no grey."[7] John speaks with a tone of authority and finality based on experience ("we have seen," 1:1). And yet there is a paternal tenderness about the epistle that makes the reader want to pause and meditate over the great truths being declared. Concerning this combination of tenderness and authority, Merrill Tenney writes, "The mellowness of the teaching . . . is not to be confused with vagueness of belief or with theological indecision."[8]

F.W. Farrar has written this accurate appraisal of the epistle's style:

> It is a style absolutely unique, supremely original, and full of charm and sweetness. Under the semblance of extreme simplicity, it hides unfathomable depths. It is to a great extent intelligible to the youngest child, to the humblest Christian; yet to enter into its full meaning exceeds the power of the deepest theologian.[9]

F. Place Among the New Testament Epistles

Twenty-one of the twenty-seven New Testament books are epistles, or letters. This type of writing, with its personal characteristics, is a natural follow-up to the historical type represented by the four gospels and Acts. As the Christian church was expanding geographically in the first decades after the day of Pentecost (Acts 2), communication from individual to individual, from group to group, and from individual to group was usually by letter. The characteristic common to all the New Testament epistles was the spiritual bond in Christ between the writer and the reader(s). This was a personal, intimate relationship, so the epistle was an appropriate channel for sharing personal testimony and delivering exhortations and commands, in addition to interpreting the grand truths of the gospel.

Eight of the twenty-one New Testament epistles do not bear the name of Paul as author. These are: Hebrews, James, 1 and 2 Peter, 1, 2, and 3 John, and Jude.[10] Of these, all but Hebrews have

7. W. Graham Scroggie, *Know Your Bible, A Brief Introduction to the Scriptures,* vol. 2, *The New Testament* (London: Pickering & Inglis, n.d.). p. 346.
8. Tenney, p. 381.
9. F.W. Farrar, *The Early Days of Christianity* (New York: Funk & Wagnalls, n.d.), pp. 520-21.
10. Whether or not Paul wrote Hebrews is still a disputed question. The epistle itself makes no explicit reference to authorship.

traditionally been classified as general epistles, a designation that only loosely refers to contents, destination, or both. Some prefer to use the classification "non-Pauline epistles."[11] J. Sidlow Baxter classifies the epistles into these three groups:[12]

9 Christian church epistles (Romans to 2 Thessalonians)
9 Hebrew Christian epistles (Hebrews to Revelation)
4 pastoral and personal epistles (1 Timothy to Philemon)

The reader may want to pursue this study further by referring to commentaries and introductory books on the epistles.

II. SURVEY OF 1 JOHN

We have been studying the *background* of 1 John in order to appreciate the reason for its being written and to anticipate some of the ways in which we may apply it to our own lives. For, if 1 John was applicable in the first century, it is applicable in the twentieth century. The Word of God is everliving, always contemporary, for the simple reason that God does not change and the basic needs of mankind remain the same throughout the ages.

Now we move to a study of the *text* of 1 John. This study is one of survey, or overview—looking at the large emphases and movements in the epistle in general. Beginning with the next lesson, we will analyze in detail each of the smaller parts of the book.

A. A First Reading

Here are suggestions in connection with your first reading of this epistle:

1. Prepare mind and heart to search diligently for all the grand truths that God would have you learn in this study. Humbly ask God to reveal Himself to you in a fresh, vivid way as you examine the Bible text. Maintain an attitude of dependency on the Holy Spirit's enlightenment throughout your study of this epistle and the ones that follow.

2. Mark new paragraph divisions in your Bible beginning at these verses:
1:1, 5, 8
2:1, 3, 7, 12, 15, 18, 20, 22, 24, 26, 28
3:1, 4, 11, 19

---

11. For example, D. Edmond Hiebert's book, cited earlier in this lesson, is titled *An Introduction to the Non-Pauline Epistles.*
12. J. Sidlow Baxter, *Explore the Book* (Grand Rapids: Zondervan, n.d.).

4:1, 7, 13, 17
5:1, 4, 6, 9, 13, 14, 18

3. Keep pencil or pen in hand as you read, for marking your Bible and recording observations.

4. Have a sheet of paper available for recording observations.

5. Now read the five chapters in one sitting. If possible, read the book aloud. As you read, do not tarry over details. Seek rather to catch the large emphases of the epistle.

6. You may want to underline words and phrases that appear prominent during this first reading. You will do more of this in the later stages of study.

7. After you have completed this reading, ask yourself these two questions: What is the tone or atmosphere of this epistle? and, What main point is John trying to get across? If you cannot arrive at an answer for either of these, try reading the epistle in a modern paraphrase such as *The Living Bible*.

B. A Second Reading

1. Now read the epistle a little more slowly, with paragraph divisions in mind. Choose a word or phrase from each paragraph to represent its contents. (We call this a paragraph title.)

2. Record the paragraph titles on Chart B, similar to the ones shown. This simple exercise will give you initial momentum as you begin your study of the text. Momentum is a must for *persistence* in the laborious but fruitful task of Bible study.

(Note: Each oblique space of Chart B represents a full *paragraph*.

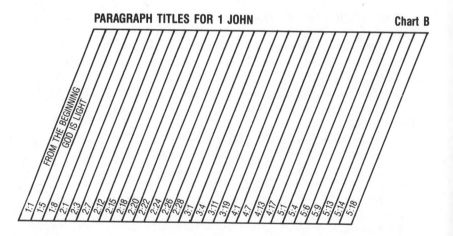

PARAGRAPH TITLES FOR 1 JOHN — Chart B

For example, the first space represents 1:1-4; the second, 1:5-7, and so forth.)

3. After you have recorded the paragraph titles, read the entire group in succession. You may not see a pattern or progression here, since the group of paragraph titles is not intended to show an outline as such; but this is a helpful exercise to review some of the highlights of John's letter.

C. Further Scanning

The exercises suggested below will help you become further acquainted with the prominent features of John's first epistle. The partially completed survey chart (Chart C) incorporates observations such as you might make in completing the exercises. Try not to refer to the chart until after you have done the exercise yourself. Such firsthand discovery is one of the best incentives for digging deep in God's mine of priceless gems.

1. Compare the opening paragraph (1:1-4) with the concluding one (5:18-21). Note, for example, such similar terms as "eternal life" in their context.

2. Scan the epistle for every reference to God. Record your observations on paper. Meditate on how much is known of God from these statements.

3. Read the following verses that refer to the Father. Record the truth and context of each reference:

1:2

_____

1:3

_____

2:1

_____

2:13

_____

2:15

_____

2:16

_____

2:22

_____

2:23

___

2:24

___

3:1

___

4:14

___

5:7

___

4. Go through the epistle and note the various contrasts that John uses to emphasize his points. As was mentioned earlier, John does not paint with the color gray—the predominant colors are the contrasting black and white. Among the contrasts you will observe are: light and darkness, truth and error, love and hate, love of the Father and love of the world, children of God and children of the devil, life and death, Christ and antichrist, believers and unbelievers. Why is the Bible written in such bold contrasts?
5. The word *know* and its cognates appear more than thirty times in the epistle. Make a study of the appearances of the phrase "we know," and record what is known in each instance:

2:3

___

2:5

___

2:29 ("ye know")

___

3:14

___

3:16 ("we perceive")

___

3:19

___

3:24

___

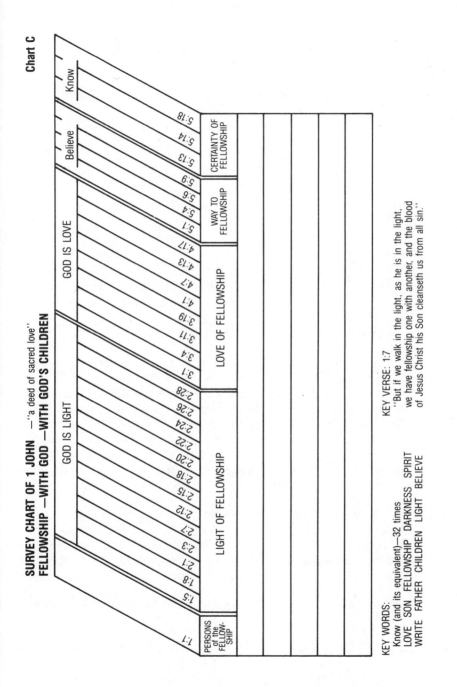

SURVEY CHART OF 1 JOHN —"a deed of sacred love"
FELLOWSHIP —WITH GOD —WITH GOD'S CHILDREN

Chart C

	GOD IS LIGHT	GOD IS LOVE			
			Believe	Know	

| 1:7 | 1:5 1:8 2:1 2:3 2:7 2:12 2:15 2:18 2:20 2:22 2:24 2:26 2:28 | 3:1 3:4 3:11 3:19 4:1 4:7 4:13 4:17 | 5:1 5:4 5:6 5:9 | 5:13 5:14 5:18 | |
| PERSONS of the FELLOW-SHIP | LIGHT OF FELLOWSHIP | LOVE OF FELLOWSHIP | WAY TO FELLOWSHIP | CERTAINTY OF FELLOWSHIP | |

KEY VERSE: 1:7
"But if we walk in the light, as he is in the light,
we have fellowship one with another, and the blood
of Jesus Christ his Son cleanseth us from all sin."

KEY WORDS:
Know (and its equivalent)—32 times
LOVE SON FELLOWSHIP DARKNESS SPIRIT
WRITE FATHER CHILDREN LIGHT BELIEVE

25

4:13

4:16 ("we have known")

5:15

5:18

5:19

5:20

---

6. Two of the grandest statements of the epistle are "God is light" (1:5) and "God is love" (4:8, 16). See how these two themes are referred to throughout the book. A closer study of these will be made in later lessons.

7. Observe where and how John refers to false teaching in his epistle.

8. What are some of the main themes of this epistle? Choose the one you think is the prominent one. On the basis of this, make a title for the epistle, and choose a key verse that reflects this theme.

9. Various attempts have been made to outline this epistle.[13] Most students of this book agree that an outline is not obvious because John's approach is not logical and argumentative but contemplative. Having stated his theme in the opening paragraph (1:1-4), John then proceeds to support the theme in various ways, item added to item, until he arrives at the conclusion of his letter (5:13-21).

Though an outline, as such, is difficult to detect in the core of the epistle (1:5–5:12), one cannot help but feel that John reaches a turning point at 3:1, where he wants to pursue the subject of fellowship from a slightly different vantage point. Read chapter 2 again, and then read 3:1ff., to see if there appears to you to be a

---

13. Such variety is evidenced by these possible breakdowns in the structure of the epistle:

> Twofold: 1:5–2:27; 2:28–5:5
> Threefold: 1:1–2:11; 2:12–4:6; 4:7–5:21
> Fourfold: 1:5–2:11; 2:12-28; 2:29–3:22; 3:33–5:17
> Fivefold: 1:5–2:11; 2:12-27; 2:28–3:24a; 3:24b–4:21; 5:1-21
> (Cf. James Moffat, *An Introduction to the Literature of the New Testament,* 1949 reprint, p. 584).

turning point at 3:1. Note the outline on *fellowship* shown on Chart C. This may suggest outlines on other subjects which you will want to develop in this survey study. For example, try making an outline on the subject "What the Christian Life Is."[14] Blank spaces on chart C can be used to record such outlines.

10. Study the other parts of Chart C if you have not already done so. Read the Bible text to observe how the last two segments (5:1-12 and 5:13-21) focus on the key words *"believe"* and *know*.

11. Note the key words shown on Chart C. Add to the list other words and phrases that you may have observed in your study thus far. Keep these words in mind for further study in later lessons of the manual.

SOME REVIEW QUESTIONS

See how many of the following you can complete without referring back to the pages of the lesson.

1. What evidence points to the fact that John was the author of the fourth gospel *and* 1 John?

2. Where and when did John write his first epistle? How old was he at the time? Justify your answers.

3. To whom may John have written this epistle? Did he know his readers intimately?

4. What were the needs of John's readers, and how did he attempt to help them in these?

5. Describe the epistle as to its form and style. In these respects compare it with an epistle like Romans.

6. For what specific reasons do you think God included 1 John in the New Testament canon? Does this epistle contribute something to the New Testament not given by any of the other twenty-six books? (Understandably, a general knowledge of the contents of all the New Testament books is a prerequisite for answering this question.)

7. From your survey study, what would you say is the main theme of 1 John? Cite a key verse supporting this.

8. What are some of the key words and phrases of the epistle?

9. What is the tone or atmosphere of the book? Does this throw any light on John's purpose in writing?

10. What are two of the grandest statements of the epistle? How much is the world in need of hearing these truths today?

14. Such an outline by one author is: (1) A Joyful Life, (2) A Victorious Life, (3) A Guarded Life, (4) A Life of Knowledge (Robert Lee, *The Outlined Bible* [New York: Revell, n.d.]).

Lesson 3

Persons of the Fellowship

The center of John's message is not a theological system or religious creed but a person—Jesus Christ. The apostle early establishes this in the opening verses of his gospel and his first epistle. In the gospel he writes, "In the beginning was the Word [Jesus]" (John 1:1). Now in the epistle, in a similar temporal setting of "the beginning," he writes, "That . . . which we have seen [Jesus] . . . declare we unto you" (1 John 1:1-3).

John also has much to say in his epistle concerning God the Father, whom he introduces in this opening paragraph (1:2-3).

And when the apostle thinks about how Jesus the Son and God the Father are related to believers like himself, the first grand truth that comes to his mind is that of *fellowship*. These are the *persons* of the fellowship. And such is the inspiration behind the glowing words of 1:1-4, which we shall now analyze in detail.

I. PREPARATION FOR STUDY

1. Read John 1:1-18 and 20:30-31. Where is Jesus first named in 1:1-18? Observe how He is the prominent figure throughout the segment. Note references to *life* in both passages. What is John referring to by the phrase "in the beginning"? Keep these words and phrases in mind as you analyze the passage.

2. Acquaint yourself with the surrounding context of 1 John 1:1-4 by reading any one of these larger units: 1:1-10; 1:1–2:2; 1:1–2:6.

3. Throughout your analysis of this passage and the ones that follow, observe even the smallest of details. John's style is to compact much into a small space. Be aware of this, and you will find that the more intently you look, the more you will see. Depend on the Spirit for help in interpreting what you see, and surrender

your will to God as you apply to your own life the truths of the Bible text.

II. ANALYSIS

Paragraph to be analyzed: 1:1-4
This paragraph is John's introduction to his epistle. It can therefore rightly be analyzed as a unit by itself, which we have chosen to do for this lesson. (It can also be profitably studied as part of a larger segment, such as 1:1–2:2.)

A. General Analysis

1. Read the four verses of the paragraphs. How many sentences are there in the King James Version? Read verse 1 immediately followed by verse 3. Observe that all of verse 2 is a parenthesis in the King James Version. Check with other versions (e.g., *Berkeley*; *Today's English Version;* these read verse 2 as though it were not a parenthesis. Why does the King James Version regard the verse as parenthetical? (Punctuation was not a part of the original autographs. It is included in Bibles to facilitate reading and study.)

---

2. Let us look more closely at the first long sentence. Whenever a long sentence appears in the Bible text, it is helpful first to identify the "core" of the sentence. By "core" I mean the main subject, main verb, and main object. Sometimes these are not easily detected, as is the case for 1:1-3. Read the sentence and record each of these parts:

MAIN SUBJECT:

MAIN VERB:

MAIN OBJECT:

Check your observations on this core with Chart D.
3. John chose to place his main subject ("we") and main verb ("declare") toward the end of this long sentence, thereby giving prominence to the main object ("that") by writing it as the *first* word of the sentence. What does the word "that" refer to? Does

your answer suggest why John chose to emphasize "that" by its location?

_____

_____

4. By now you have begun to see what are the emphasized truths of this paragraph and what are the interrelationships between them. This would be a good time to write out the paragraph on paper, pictorializing it by showing emphases and relationships. This procedure of study is called textual re-creation. It is simply doing on paper what one does orally when he reads aloud a passage of Scripture interpretatively (e.g., showing emphases by loudness, and relations by inflections, etc.)

Textual re-creation shows in visual forms not only *what* the text is saying but *how* it is saying it. Repetitions, comparisons, and progressions are some of the things we can pictorialize by such writing devices as indentation, underlinings, listings, arrows, and color. Chart D is a simple textual re-creation of 1:1-4, with a brief outline placed in the margin. Look at Chart D briefly; then do your own textual re-creation on a sheet of paper, within a four by six-inch rectangle. After you have completed this, continue with the study suggestions given below, aimed at helping you see emphasized truths and related truths of this paragraph.

5. Let your textual re-creation clearly show the core of the first sentence: "That . . . declare we." You have already determined what the word "that" of verse 1 refers to. If it refers to John's message, what do the verses reveal as to the *content* of the message and the *purpose* of declaring the message?

_____

_____

_____

6. Observe the progression in the first half of the paragraph. How does John relate his message to each of the following: a real person; life; eternal life? Do you see any progression here, and if so, what is the significance of it?

_____

_____

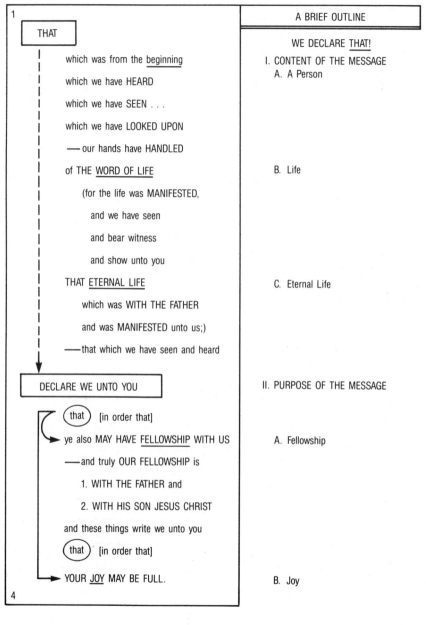

	A BRIEF OUTLINE

1

THAT

WE DECLARE THAT!

which was from the beginning

I. CONTENT OF THE MESSAGE
   A. A Person

which we have HEARD

which we have SEEN . . .

which we have LOOKED UPON

— our hands have HANDLED

of THE WORD OF LIFE   B. Life

(for the life was MANIFESTED,

and we have seen

and bear witness

and show unto you

THAT ETERNAL LIFE   C. Eternal Life

which was WITH THE FATHER

and was MANIFESTED unto us;)

——that which we have seen and heard

DECLARE WE UNTO YOU   II. PURPOSE OF THE MESSAGE

that [in order that]

ye also MAY HAVE FELLOWSHIP WITH US   A. Fellowship

——and truly OUR FELLOWSHIP is

1. WITH THE FATHER and

2. WITH HIS SON JESUS CHRIST

and these things write we unto you

that [in order that]

YOUR JOY MAY BE FULL.   B. Joy

4

31

7. What are key repeated words and phrases of the paragraph? Meditate on the truths of these.

_____

_____

8. Observe the two clauses of purpose beginning with the word "that" (meaning "in order that"). What two purposes for declaring the gospel of Jesus does John cite?

_____

Think much about these. In what sense are they "musts" for the healthy Christian life?

_____

9. Look for time references in this paragraph, and probe their meaning. What is Jesus' relation to each one?

_____

_____

B. Verse Analysis

1. *Verse 1*. Note the two phrases "we have seen" and "with our eyes." Why did John add this second phrase to the first?

_____

On the word "handled," compare Luke 24:39. (Cf. also John 20:27.) Do you think John was thinking of the event recorded here?

_____

2. *Verse 2*. What is meant by "that eternal life, which was with the Father?" Is this a reference to Jesus' being with the Father? If so, what does this teach about Jesus' nature?

_____

_____

What is eternal life?

_____

_____

3. *Verse 3.* "Our fellowship is with the Father, and with his Son Jesus Christ." Observe that this verse teaches that the Son and the
Father are two distinct Persons. Does it teach the deity of Christ? If
so, how?

_____

_____

We have already observed in our studies that the subject of fellowship is a main subject of this epistle. How was John's fellowship
with his readers related to his declaring the message of Christ?

_____

_____

What do you think is involved in fellowship with God?

_____

_____

How is the fellowship of two believers with each other related to
each one's fellowship with God?

_____

_____

What do you expect would be some of the conditions for main-
taining such fellowship with God?

_____

_____

_____

_____

Answers to these questions from the Bible text will come as you
study further in the epistle.

III. NOTES

1. "That which was from the beginning" (1:1. In John 1:1, the
phrase is "In the beginning was the Word." There John was teaching who Jesus was *before* the foundation of the world and *at* the
foundation of the world. In this first verse of the epistle, he is writ-

ing of that which has been true of Jesus since that time of creation,[1] John's choice of the neuter phrase "that which" instead of "him who" does not draw attention away from the *Person* Jesus. John's burden in this epistle is multifold. For example, he wishes to speak about (1) Jesus the God-Man; (2) what He accomplished; and (3) what this means to the believer. In view of this, we can understand John's writing "we declare *that*" (a word referring to the various truths, *including* the Person of Jesus) rather than "we declare *Him*."

2. "Our fellowship is with the Father, and with his Son Jesus Christ" (1:3). This simple statement teaches some profound truths. Among these are:

a. The Father and the Son are two distinct Persons.

b. The Father and the Son are one in essence and equal in dignity.

c. A believer is brought into intimate association with the Father and the Son. No human words can adequately convey all that this involves for the believer.

3. "That your joy may be full" (1:4). The word translated "full" may be more correctly translated as "fulfilled" or "complete." Read these other verses written by John that contain the same Greek word: John 3:29; 7:8; 12:38; 15:11; 2 John 12.

Concerning the phrase "your *joy*," some of the best ancient manuscripts read "our joy," a translation used by most modern versions (e.g., *Berkeley*). Actually, the basic application is the same. (Read 2 John 12 for a similar wording by John.)

IV. FURTHER ADVANCED STUDY

1. At some time during your study of 1 John you will want to make a topical study of the word *fellowship* (Greek *koinonia*) as it is used in the New Testament. (It is interesting to note that this word is mainly found in the Pauline writings, 1 John being the exception.) Use an exhaustive concordance to locate the various places where the word is used.[2] Among the passages that you will want to consult are: Acts 2:42; 1 Corinthians 1:9; 2 Corinthians 8:4; Philippians 1:5; 3:10.

2. The phrase "the Word of life" is a suggestive one.[3] Think of all the possible shades of meaning intended by it.

1. See Kenneth S. Wuest, *In These Last Days*, pp. 87-88.
2. Two standard works are: James Strong, *The Exhaustive Concordance of the Bible*, and Robert Young, *Analytical Concordance to the Bible*.
3. The Greek of this verse reads, "The Word of life," a wording that appears nowhere else in the Bible.

V. APPLICATIONS

1. What gifts of God to the believer are mentioned in this paragraph?

_____

_____

_____

_____

If these are yours, how grateful are you for having received them?
2. What truths about the Father and His Son are taught in these verses?

_____

_____

_____

What bearing do these have on Christian living?
3. What tone of assurance do you sense in these verses?
In what ways is assurance a key to the victorious Christian life?

_____

_____

_____

_____

VI. WORDS TO PONDER

We have seen it, and bear witness (1:2).
It is one thing to see; it is another to see *plus* witness.

Lesson 4

Conditions for Fellowship with God

Opening his epistle, John introduced the grand subject of fellowship among Christians and with God and Christ. Now the apostle identifies the conditions or requirements of that fellowship, so that there will be no question in the minds of his readers how one can enjoy the full blessings that such a fellowship brings.

I. PREPARATION FOR STUDY

1. Review the first paragraph (1:1-4), especially for what it teaches about fellowship. Keep in mind that the word *fellowship* (from the Greek root *koinos*, "common") denotes a group of two or more members who *share something in common*.

2. Read the passage of this lesson in one or two modern versions. Note especially how the word "propitiation" (2:2) is translated or paraphrased.

3. Prepare a work sheet with a four-by-nine-inch rectangle drawn on it, similar to that of Chart E. Make new paragraphs at 1:5; 1:8; and 2:1. Write out a textual re-creation of these three paragraphs, such as was done in Lesson 3. It will amaze you how many new truths you begin to see in the Bible text once you begin to pictorialize the text by showing *emphases* and *relations*.

4. Because sin is an important subject in this passage, have clear in your mind just what sin is. With the help of outside sources, refer to other verses in the Bible that define or describe sin (e.g., Rom. 6-7). A classic definition of sin is given in 1 John 3:4, where we read that "sin is the transgression of the law" (that is, God's law).

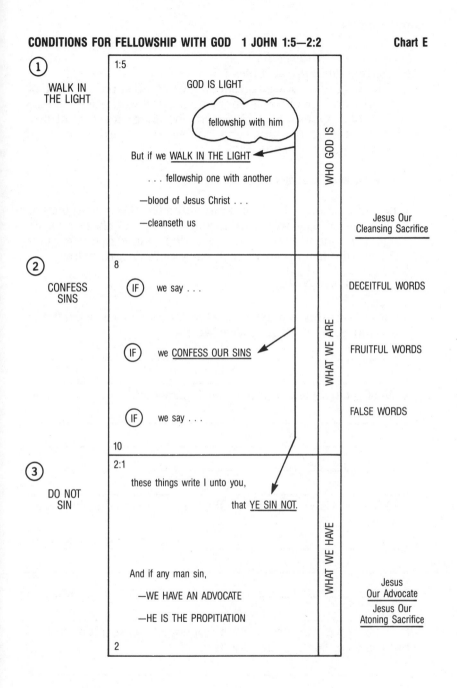

① WALK IN THE LIGHT

1:5

GOD IS LIGHT

fellowship with him

But if we WALK IN THE LIGHT

. . . fellowship one with another

—blood of Jesus Christ . . .

—cleanseth us

WHO GOD IS

Jesus Our Cleansing Sacrifice

② CONFESS SINS

8

IF   we say . . .   DECEITFUL WORDS

IF   we CONFESS OUR SINS   FRUITFUL WORDS

IF   we say . . .   FALSE WORDS

10

WHAT WE ARE

③ DO NOT SIN

2:1

these things write I unto you,

that YE SIN NOT.

And if any man sin,

—WE HAVE AN ADVOCATE

—HE IS THE PROPITIATION

2

WHAT WE HAVE

Jesus Our Advocate

Jesus Our Atoning Sacrifice

II. ANALYSIS

Segment to be analyzed: 1:5–2:2
Paragraph divisions: at verses 1:5, 8; 2:1
In following the study suggestions given below, record your observations and conclusions on your analytical work sheet whenever possible. (Questions 1-8 concern the entire segment of three paragraphs. The questions that follow them narrow the study down to paragraphs and verses.)

A. General Analysis

1. Read the passage slowly and carefully a few times, marking your Bible to show key words and phrases. Most of these probably caught your attention when you recorded your textual re-creation.
2. What is the main point of each paragraph? Record below
1:5-7 :
1:8-10 :
2:1-2 :
3. How does this outline represent the gist of each paragraph: Who God Is; What We Are; What We Have?

_____

_____

4. What is taught about Jesus in each paragraph?

_____

_____

_____

5. What conditions for fellowship are cited in the three paragraphs?

_____

_____

_____

6. What is the purpose of John's opening this segment with the profound declaration that God is light?

_____

_____

What does fellowship have to do with this truth?

7. Observe every reference to sin in the passage. What synonyms and other related words give a description of what sin is?

For example, in what way does the symbol "darkness" depict sin? Answer this by first determining what darkness is in the natural world.

8. What various truths are taught here concerning God's gracious work for man in his predicament of sin?

B. Paragraph Analysis

1. *Paragraph 1:5-7: Who God Is.* Observe how the subject of fellowship is treated in these verses. The following diagram illustrates the differences between darkness-walkers and light-walkers.

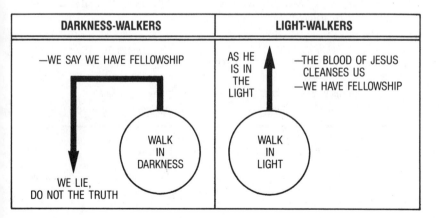

DARKNESS-WALKERS	LIGHT-WALKERS
—WE SAY WE HAVE FELLOWSHIP	AS HE IS IN THE LIGHT —THE BLOOD OF JESUS CLEANSES US —WE HAVE FELLOWSHIP
WALK IN DARKNESS	WALK IN LIGHT
WE LIE, DO NOT THE TRUTH	

How is genuine fellowship with God contrasted with nonexistent fellowship? Why would a person falsely claim fellowship with God?

Compare the phrases "fellowship with him" (v. 6) and "fellowship one with another" (v. 7). The latter phrase refers either to a fellowship among believers or to a fellowship involving believers and God. Which of these interpretations do you think is suggested by the context?

Observe that the phrase "the blood of Jesus Christ his Son cleanseth us from all sin" immediately follows the phrase "we have fellowship one with another." What does Christ's cleansing blood have to do with this fellowship?

2. *Paragraph 1:8-10: What We Are.* What is the key repeated word of this paragraph?

Note the opening word of each verse. All the verses are about man's speaking: deceitful words (v. 8), fruitful words (v. 9), and false words (v. 10). Compare the three clauses of the first and last verses, listed below:

verse 8	verse 10
If we say that we have no sin, ⟶	If we say that we have not sinned,
we deceive ourselves, ⟶	we make him a liar,
and the truth is not in us. ⟶	and his word is not in us.

What is the bright message of the central verse?

Who is "he" in verse 9 and "him" in verse 10?

_____

_____

God's forgiving us our sins (v. 9) is based on what divine attributes?[1] What is the difference between each of the two attributes cited?

_____

_____

3. *Paragraph 2:1-2: What We Have.* Does verse 1 teach that a believer can attain sinless perfection in this life? If not, justify the strong wording "that ye sin not."

_____

God's gracious provision for sinners is taught by two words in this paragraph:
    (a) *Advocate (2:1).* What is the function of an advocate?

_____

_____

Does Christ automatically function as the believer's advocate on the occasion of a sin, or must the believer do something first (cf. 1:9)?

_____

_____

    (b) *Propitiation (2:2, cf. 4:10).* Compare other versions for help in understanding what is meant by this word. For example, the Williams version reads, "And He is Himself the atoning sacrifice for our sins." In what sense is Jesus' propitiation applicable to the whole world (2:2b)? Is He an advocate for the whole world?

_____

_____

4. Before leaving this part of your analysis, read the entire passage again (1:5–2:2), and reach some conclusions as to what John's purpose was in writing these paragraphs. How much of this passage is doctrine? command? exhortation?

---

1. Observe here that who God is is basic to what God does. That is, His *works* are dependent on His *person.*

III. NOTES

1. "God is light" (1:5). Of this Marvin R. Vincent writes, "Not *a* light, nor *the* light, with reference to created beings, as *the light of men; the light of the world*, but simply and absolutely *God is light*, in His very nature."[2] Read Genesis 1:3-5, and observe that physical light was the creation of the first of the six creative days.

2. "We have fellowship one with another" (1:7). Opinion is divided as to who are intended by John as the members of this fellowship: either (a) believers with believers,[3] or (b) believers with God.[4]

3. "We have no sin" (1:8). *The Wycliffe Bible Commentary* states: "The phrase *to have sin* is peculiar to John in the NT (cf. John 9:41; 15:22, 24; 19:11). It refers to the nature, principle, or root of sin, rather than to the act."[5] The phrase "have not sinned" of verse 10 refers to the *act* of sin.

4. "That ye sin not" (2:1). This command is given in the ultimate degree, even though a total fulfillment of it is impossible for a believer *in this life*. Not to put the command in these strong terms would support a reading that could never originate with God, such as, "These things write I unto you, that ye sin only occasionally."

5. "We have an advocate" (2:1). The Greek word (*parakletos*) translated "advocate" literally means "one called to one's side," or a helper. In New Testament days the word was used in a court of justice to denote a legal assistant, or counsel, for the defense. John applies the title to Jesus as one who pleads a believer's cause before his heavenly Father.

6. "He is the propitiation for our sins" (2:2). The idea here is not that of appeasing an angry God but of satisfying God's conditions required for restoration of fellowship between man and God. The atoning death of Christ made this restoration possible. The *Berkeley Version* translates this phrase thus: "He is Himself an atoning sacrifice for our sins." Compare the readings of other versions.

---

2. Marvin R. Vincent, *Word Studies in the New Testament*, 2:312.
3. Westcott says, "The supposition that *met allelon* ("with one another") means 'we with God and God with us' is against the apostolic form of language (John xx. 17), and also against the general form of St. John's argument, for he takes the fellowship of Christians as the visible sign and correlative of fellowship with God: iv. 7, 12. Comp. iii. 11, 23" (*The Epistle* of St. John, p. 21).
4. Kenneth S. Wuest says that the theme of the epistle and the immediate context indicate that the "we" are God and the believer (*In These Last Days*, p. 102). I am inclined to agree that the immediate context so indicates.
5. Charles C. Ryrie, "I, II, III John," in *The Wycliffe Bible Commentary*, p. 1467.

IV. FURTHER ADVANCED STUDY

Make a topical study of various aspects of sin. An encyclopedia on Bible words will be of help in suggesting various areas of study on the subject.

V. APPLICATIONS

List all the things mentioned in the eight verses of this passage that have a bearing on Christian living. Observe how uncomplicated and genuine a Christian's life should be.

VI. WORDS TO PONDER

Without shedding of blood is no remission (Heb. 9:22).

But if we confess our sins to Him, He can be depended on to forgive us our sins and to cleanse us from every wrong. And it is perfectly proper for God to do this for us because Christ died to wash away our sins (1 John 1:9, *The Living Bible*).

> There is a fountain filled with blood
> Drawn from Immanuel's veins;
> And sinners, plunged beneath that flood,
> Lose all their guilty stains.
>   (William Cooper)

Lesson 5

Abiding in Christ

Up to now, John has established Christians' forgiveness of sins and fellowship with God and believers. At this point, the apostle anticipates a question that his reader could rightly ask, How can I *know* if I am in this fellowship with God? John's answer to the question is simple yet strong:

> Hereby we do *know* that we know him,
> *if we keep his commandments* (2:3).

The verses that follow are an expansion of this theme, teaching what kind of a walk describes the Christian who is abiding in Christ, knowing Him personally and experientially.

I. PREPARATION FOR STUDY

1. Set up on a piece of paper (8 1/2 by 11 inches) a work sheet similar to the ones used in the previous lessons, on which you can develop an analytical chart as you study. This work sheet is basically of two parts: (1) words of the Bible text recorded inside a 4-by-9-inch rectangle; and (2) your own words (e.g., outlines) recorded in the margins. (See example on p. 42.)
How you choose to organize your observations on this work sheet is up to you. (The analytical charts shown in this manual illustrate one method.) The important thing is for you to *record* what you see. *Jot it down* is the byword here.
2. For review, read 1:1–2:2, and observe that there is no specific reference thus far in the epistle to the *assurance* of abiding in Christ. (The first appearance of the key word "know" is at 2:3.) But observe that the tone of 1:1–2:2 is nevertheless authoritative and final, leaving no question as to the truth of the facts of the gospel (e.g., "we have seen;" "the life was manifested").

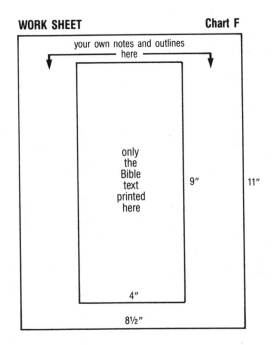

II. ANALYSIS

Segment to be analyzed: 2:3-17
Paragraph divisions: at verses 3, 7, 12, 15
(Note: Whenever possible, record your observations and conclusions on your work sheet.)

A. General Analysis

1. Read the four paragraphs to determine what is the theme or main point of each. What is so different about the third paragraph (2:12-14)? Can you suggest a reason why John included it in this context?

_____

_____

2. Underline in your Bible the four appearances of the word "abideth."
How is the word used in each case? Record below:
"abideth in him" (v. 6):

_____

45

"abideth in the light" (v. 10):

"Abideth in you" (v. 14):

"Abideth for ever" (v. 17):

Note the main topical study, "Abiding in Christ," on Chart G.

3. In what sense does the phrase "abideth in him" (2:6) express the thought of "fellowship" (2:3)? (Recall your earlier study of the word *fellowship*.)

4. Read the four paragraphs again, noting each reference to Christian living, or action, such as "keep his commandments" (2:3). Observe that the segment opens with a reference to works ("keep," v. 3) and closes on the same note ("doeth," v. 17).

5. Which paragraphs refer to evil, and in what ways? Mark every such word or phrase in your Bible, and it will be apparent how much emphasis John places on this subject in this segment.

---

6. Note the reference to "Father" and "God" in the passage.[1] Is Christ named in the text? Is 2:6*b* a reference to Christ?

---

7. How many times does the phrase "he that saith" appear in the text? What is the point in each case? Recall references to this subject earlier in the epistle.

---

8. Before moving on to a more detailed analysis of each paragraph and its individual verses, work more on your work sheet to develop outlines and other studies of the segment as a whole. (A few

---

1. The term "Father" appears in John's writings more often than in the three synoptic gospels combined.

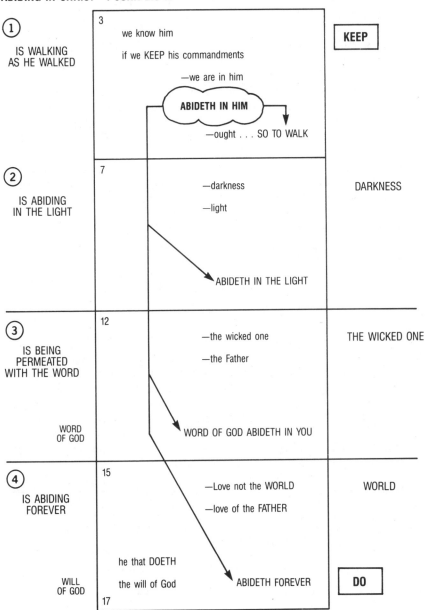

①

**IS WALKING
AS HE WALKED**

3

we know him

if we KEEP his commandments

—we are in him

ABIDETH IN HIM

—ought . . . SO TO WALK

KEEP

②

**IS ABIDING
IN THE LIGHT**

7

—darkness

—light

ABIDETH IN THE LIGHT

DARKNESS

③

**IS BEING
PERMEATED
WITH THE WORD**

12

—the wicked one

—the Father

WORD
OF GOD

WORD OF GOD ABIDETH IN YOU

THE WICKED ONE

④

**IS ABIDING
FOREVER**

15

—Love not the WORLD

—love of the FATHER

he that DOETH

WILL
OF GOD

the will of God   ABIDETH FOREVER

17

WORLD

DO

examples of these are shown on Chart G.) This exercise will give you a better *feel* for the entire segment and will help you recognize the meaning and importance of the individual truths as they appear in the sentences.

B. Paragraph Analysis

1. *Paragraph 2:3-6*
"Hereby we do know that we know him" (v. 3). One Greek word (*ginosko*)[2] is translated "know" both times in this verse and in all the other appearances in this segment except at verse 11. Compare "hereby we do know that we know" (v. 3) with "hereby know we that we are in him" (v. 5).
Who is the "him" of verse 3? To answer this, compare the preceding verse (2:2), and follow the third person pronoun through verses 3 to 6 to the reference "even as he walked" (2:6).

What does it mean to "know him [Christ]"?

The phrase "love of God" (2:5) is probably intended to involve an objective genitive, meaning the Christian's love toward God. (Cf. 2:15 and 5:3. Read these verses also in modern versions.)
If there is a chronological order involved in the following phrases as related to a believer's experience or position, list them in the correct order: "keep his commandments" (v. 3); "abideth in him" (v. 6): "love of [toward] God perfected" (v. 5.

"Even as he walked" (2:6). What qualities of Christ's life especially come to mind as you read these words?

---

2. This is the word from which "gnostic" is derived. The Gnostics of John's day claimed they had secret knowledge of God. John here says that a man's walk will reveal if he knows God personally.

2. *Paragraph 2:7-11*

Christ's "commandments" (2:3), or precepts, were equated with His "word" in 2:5. Now John uses the singular word "commandment" (2:7-8). What may John have meant by this commandment? Could it have been the commandment of *love*, which is the subject of the last half of this paragraph?[3] What may be meant by the phrase "from the beginning" (2:7)?

_____

_____

In what ways is Christ's commandment old *yet* new?

_____

_____

What truths are taught about darkness and light in this paragraph?

_____

_____

_____

Why is so much prominence given to love among Christians? Relate this to the epistle's theme of fellowship.

_____

_____

_____

3. *Paragraph 2:12-14*

Write out the lists of this paragraph so that you can compare the statements more easily. Refer to the Notes for explanations of some phrases in the paragraph. Associate each particular group with what is said about each (e.g., young men overcoming "the wicked one"). Who is "the wicked one"?

_____

_____

Think again about why John included this paragraph in his letter. Why did he place it in this location?

_____

_____

3. This is the view of Henry Alford, *The Greek Testament*, pp. 436-37.

"For his name's sake" (2:12). In what ways is Christ's name related to our forgiveness? (Cf. 1:9.)

4. *Paragraph 2:15-17*
What is taught here about the "world"?

Read "love of the Father" (v. 15) as "love toward the Father."
Compare verse 15 with Matthew 6:24.
What is meant by each of the following (v. 16):
"lust of the flesh"

"lust of the eyes"

"pride of life"

Relate these to the first sins of the human race, recorded in Genesis 3.
What facts are contrasted, as to time, in 2:17?

III. NOTES

1. "Commandment which ye had from the beginning" (2:7). John's Christian readers had received Christ's word from the beginning of their Christian faith.

2. "The darkness is past" (2:8). This is accurately translated, "The darkness is passing away."

3. "Darkness hath blinded his eyes" (2:11). Of this, David Smith has written, "The penalty of living in the darkness is not merely that one does not see, but that one goes blind. The neglected faculty is atrophied. Compare the mole, the crustacea in the Mammoth Cave of Kentucky."[4]

4. Quoted in Kenneth S. Wuest, *In These Last Days*, p. 122.

4. "Little children" (2:12-13). In verse 12 the Greek word is *teknia*, representing kinship. So John writes this verse as to those spiritually related to him. In verse 13 the Greek word is *paidia*, suggesting subordination, or listening to instruction. Wuest paraphrases this verse thus: "I write to you, little children under instruction, because you have come to know the Father experientially, with the present result that you are possessors of that knowledge."[5]

5. "I write" (2:12). The present tense of this phrase in verses 12 and 13 refers to John's immediate act of writing. The past tense "I have written" (or "I wrote") refers to the reader's act of reading the completed writing.[6]

6. "Love not the world" (2:15). This is not a command to love not the world of men, but to love not that system that is hostile to God.[7] On this Wuest writes:

> **Kosmos** is . . . the ordered system of which Satan is the head, his fallen angels and demons are his emissaries, and the unsaved of the human race are his subjects, together with those purposes, pursuits, pleasures, practices and places where God is not wanted. Much in this world-system is religious, cultured, refined, and intellectual. But it is anti-God and anti-Christ.[8]

IV. FURTHER ADVANCED STUDY

Important words of this passage suggested for further study are:

1. know (Two different words in the Greek are used by John: *oida* and *ginosko*. A concordance will direct you to the verses where each is used. Study especially John's use of the words.)
2. abide
3. world
4. love
5. Father
6. forever; everlasting

V. APPLICATIONS

1. Do you know that you are in Christ—that you are in fellowship with Him?

5. Ibid., p. 124.
6. Marvin R. Vincent, *Word Studies in the New Testament*, 2:334.
7. The Greek translated "world" is *kosmos*, an ordered system (opposite of *chaos*).
8. Wuest, p. 125.

2. Do you seek to walk even as Christ walked?

3. Do you love your Christian brothers?

4. Do you believe that Satan is an enemy to be overcome.

5. Does the Word of God abide in you?

6. Do you love the things that are in the world—that which is hostile to God?

7. What activities would you classify "worldly" because they involve lust of the flesh, lust of the eyes, and pride of life?

8. Can you say that you genuinely seek to do the will of God in your everyday living?

9. What blessings do you associate with abiding forever (2:17)?

10. How do you react to commands of Scripture directed to you?

VI. WORDS TO PONDER

The world and everything in it that men desire is passing away; but he who does what God wants lives for ever (2:17; *Today's English Version*).

Lesson 6

Antichrists and Christians

When writing of living in fellowship with God, John, a realist, would inevitably recognize a hostile domain. This domain and its environment are in direct opposition to that fellowship. This is the reason for the large space already devoted in his epistle to such subjects as sin, Satan (the "wicked one"), the world, and darkness. Now John introduces another hostile element—a personal one that he labels antichrist (Greek *antichristos*).[1] The apostle calls the enemies of Christ, as described in this passage, "antichrists." Our study of this lesson will be focused on the contrasts John makes between antichrists and Christians.

Professing Christians are not antichrists, but they are not necessarily genuine Christians of whom John writes in this passage. As you study the text, discover what marks of a genuine Christian are cited here. Also, as you analyze what is said about antichrists, identify the type of person that would be classified as an antichrist today.

I. PREPARATION FOR STUDY

1. Review your study of Lesson 5 having to do with the subject "abiding in Christ." That is background for this lesson's treatment of the same subject. Mark verse 2:24 in your Bible to read the word "abide" in three places:[2]

---

1. The word "antichrist" is used only by John in the New Testament, at these places: 1 John 2:18, 22; 4:3; 2 John 7. The prefix *anti* of the Greek may be translated either "against" or "instead of." *Zondervan Pictorial Bible Dictionary* thus states, "The word antichrist may mean either an enemy of Christ or one who usurps Christ's name and rights" (Merrill C. Tenney, ed. [Grand Rapids: Zondervan, 1963], p. 47).
2. The same Greek word (*meno*) appears at all three places in the original text.

"Let that therefore abide in you"
"from the beginning shall abide in you"
"ye also shall abide in the Son"

2. Set up on a work sheet four rectangles as shown on Chart H.
This will be the place to record observations of the text.

ANTICHRISTS AND CHRISTIANS   1 JOHN 2:18-29   **Chart H**

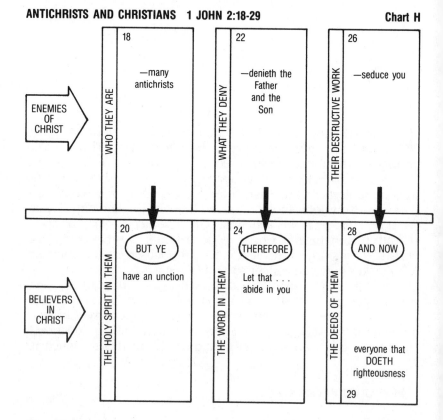

II. ANALYSIS

Segment to be analyzed: 2:18-29
Paragraph divisions: at verses 2:18, 20, 22, 24, 26, 28

    1. First mark in your Bible the paragraph divisions shown
above. Then read the passage slowly, marking key words and
phrases as you read.

    2. Observe on Chart H that the six paragraphs of this segment
appear as three groups of two paragraphs each.

    3. The three top paragraphs (2:18-19; 2:22-23; 2:26-27) refer
to enemies of Christ (e.g., "antichrists"), whereas the bottom para-

graphs are about believers in Christ, with no reference to the enemies. This arrangement by use of charts helps one to make a comparative study of those subjects.

4. Note the introductory words of each of the bottom paragraphs: "but ye"; "therefore"; "and now." Keep in mind the functions of these words as you analyze the paragraphs later on.

5. Read in your Bible each of the top paragraphs, and determine a main subject for each paragraph, related to the title "Enemies of Christ." Do the same for the bottom paragraphs, related to the title "Believers in Christ." Then compare your outlines with those shown on Chart H.

A. Enemies of Christ

The order of the following questions follows that of the outline shown on Chart H. Do not let the outline itself limit your own activity in observing and reaching conclusions.

1. *Who they are* (2:18-19)

What does the word *antichrist* suggest to you? What are the time references of verse 18? What is alluded to in the phrase "last time"? Compare this phrase with "the world passeth away" (2:17).

_____

_____

_____

Since John was living in end times (2:18),[3] and since we today are closer to the end of the world, what is the duration of the period here designated as "last time"?

_____

_____

What is the main point of verse 19?

_____

_____

List the things said about antichrists in this paragraph.

_____

_____

3. The phrase of 2:18 is literally "it is a last time."

2. *What they deny* (2:22-23)[4]

According to these verses, what do antichrists deny? In answering, keep in mind the meaning or significance of each of these references in the passage:

Jesus (see Matt. 1:21)

Christ (from *krino*, to "anoint")

John no doubt had in mind the Gnostics of his day when he wrote these words about denying the truth. This is suggested by these false views held by the Gnostics:

(1) Christ and Jesus were two distinct beings.

(2) The Christ descended upon Jesus at His baptism and departed before His death.

What is meant by the phrase "Hath not the Father?"

---

3. *Their destructive work* (2:26-27)

What reference to enemies of Christ is made in verse 26? How does this introduce the subject of *teaching* in the next verse?

Note the various references to teaching in verse 27. Is it possible that the reference "any man teach you" is to false teachers (*only*, or *besides*, teachers of the truth)? Compare 4:1-3.

Note the two appearances of "anointing" in this paragraph. The same Greek word appears in verse 20, translated in the King James Version as "unction." In all three instances the anointing is related to teaching. What is meant by this, and how is it related to the threat of false teaching (deception) cited in verse 26?

---

4. Note: The last phrase of 2:23, printed in italics in the King James Version, is really part of the original text of 1 John.

B. Believers in Christ

1. The Holy Spirit in them (2:20-21)
As observed earlier, the word "unction" (v. 20) could be translated "anointing." The picture is that of pouring lotion or ointment on an object. The applied truth is that God pours out the Holy Spirit upon a believer at the moment of new birth. From that time on the Spirit indwells the believer, so that He can perform a ministry for his benefit. One of the ministries is that of teaching (read John 16:12-15.) Observe the importance of the word "know" in 2:20-21. Why is it important to know the truth concerning God?

2. The Word in them (2:24-25)
Study carefully the following sequence in this paragraph:

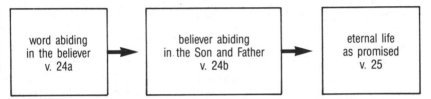

word abiding in the believer v. 24a	→	believer abiding in the Son and Father v. 24b	→	eternal life as promised v. 25

3. The deeds of them (2:28-29)
What is meant by the phrase "doeth righteousness" (v. 29)? Interpret the other truths of this paragraph in the light of this phrase. What does "at his coming" refer to?

_____

_____

III. NOTES

1. "Antichrist . . . many antichrists" (2:18). In John's day, Christians knew that a personal antichrist would one day appear in this world. The Old Testament, Jesus, and Paul's writings taught about such a personage as the "man of sin." Compare 2 Thessalonians 2:4 with Daniel 11:36-37; Revelation 13:1-8 with Daniel 7:8, 20ff.; 8:24; 11:28-30. Read also Ezekiel 38-39; Zechariah 12-14; Matthew 24:15, 24; Mark 13:22; 2 Thessalonians 2:1-12; Revelation 17:8.

2. "Jesus is the Christ" (2:22). The word "Jesus" transliterates the Greek *Iesous,* which in turn transliterates the Hebrew name pronounced "Jehoshua." This Hebrew name means literally "Jehovah saves." Of this Wuest writes:

> Thus, in the name "Jesus" there is contained the doctrines of the deity, humanity and vicarious atonement of the Person who

bears that name. Only Jehovah could offer a sacrifice which would satisfy the demands of His holy law which the human race broke. But that sacrifice had to include within itself human nature without its sin, for deity in itself could not die, and deity acting as Priest for the sinner must partake of the nature of the individual on whose behalf He officiates.[5]

The Greek word *Christos* is derived from *krino* (meaning "to anoint"). Christ is thus the anointed one, the Messiah, sent to the world to redeem mankind.

IV. FURTHER ADVANCED STUDY

Subjects recommended for extended study are: eternal life, the second coming of Christ, and Antichrist.

V. APPLICATIONS

The subject of antichrists is a main subject of this passage. Recall from the passage what basic truths concerning Christ and God are denied by such men. Is this spirit of denial prevalent in Christendom today? What do modern liberal theologians, who profess to be Christians, deny about Christ? What stand and action do you think born-again Christians ("born of him," 2:29) should take in view of the alarming "antichrist" movement in the world today?

VI. WORDS TO PONDER

Who is the liar if it is not the denier that Jesus is the Christ? (2:22, *Berkeley*).

VII. SUMMARY EXERCISE ON 1:1–2:29

We have arrived at the end of a main division in the first epistle of John. (Observe on Chart C the new division, which begins at 3:1.) The theme "God Is Light" is a major theme for 1:1–2:29. Read these two chapters again, with this theme in mind. Recall your analytical studies made up to this point, and try to discover new insights into the meaning of this profound truth, that *God is light.*

---

5. Kenneth S. Wuest, *In These Last Days*, p. 134.

Beloved Sons of God

At this point in the epistle John begins to emphasize more strongly and frequently that God is love. Up to this point the emphasis has been mainly that *God is light*. (See survey Chart C.) See 4:8 and 4:16 for the two appearances of the simple yet profound declaration "God is love." (Recall the declaration "God is light" made in 1:5.)

As if to command utmost attention from his readers to the words he is about to write, John begins this new section with the exclamatory "Behold." "Look–stand in awe and consider," writes John, "what manner of love the Father hath bestowed upon us!" As we begin our study of this inspiring chapter, it will help us immeasurably to catch the spirit of these opening words of John, pondering this tremendous truth of God's love to us.

I. PREPARATION FOR STUDY

1. The word "beloved" appears for the first time in John's epistle at 3:2. With the help of a concordance, make a study of this word as it appears in various contexts in the New Testament. It is the same word used of Christ's relationship to His Father in Matthew 3:17. Why is this word such an appropriate one to identify believers in Christ?

_____

_____

2. To view the organization of this chapter into four paragraphs, see Chart I. Mark the paragraph divisions in your Bible.

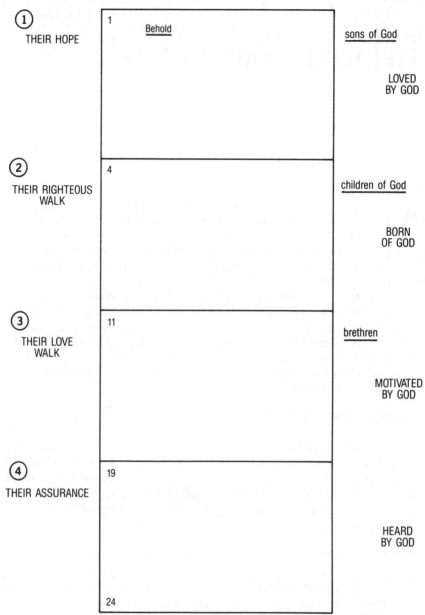

(1) THEIR HOPE

1 Behold

sons of God

LOVED
BY GOD

(2) THEIR RIGHTEOUS
WALK

4

children of God

BORN
OF GOD

(3) THEIR LOVE
WALK

11

brethren

MOTIVATED
BY GOD

(4) THEIR ASSURANCE

19

HEARD
BY GOD

24

II. ANALYSIS

Segment to be analyzed: 3:1-24
Paragraph divisions: at verses 1, 4, 11, 19

A. General Analysis

Read through the chapter, keeping the paragraph divisions in mind. Record below the main theme of each paragraph:

3:1-3

3:4-10

3:11-18

3:19-24

Read the chapter again, looking for references to the following subjects:
(1) different Persons of the Trinity
(2) God's family (e.g., "brethren")
(3) believers as objects of God's working (e.g., "born of God")
(4) descriptions of believers in each paragraph

B. Paragraph Analysis

1. *Paragraph 3:1-3*
Compare the opening reference to love ("love . . . upon us") with the closing reference to hope ("hope in him"). What is hope?

What is "this hope" in the context of 3:2-3?

John was overwhelmed by the truth that he was called a son of God (3:1). Do you share this reaction with John? What are the implications of this relationship—"sons of God"?

Compare "is born of him" (2:29) and "we shall be like him" (3:2).

_____

_____

What future event is John talking about in verse 2?

_____

_____

How does he relate this in verse 3 to the present?

_____

_____

How can a son of God purify himself as Christ is pure?

_____

_____

Compare the contexts of the phrase "when he shall appear" in 2:28-29 and 3:2-3.

_____

2. *Paragraph 3:4-10*
Note the two groups of people mentioned in verse 10a. (Cf. Eph. 2:3.) Record in the columns below what is said about each group. Do the two groups together constitute all of mankind?

children of God	children of the devil

Much is taught about sin in this paragraph. Such phrases as "whosoever is born of God doth not commit sin" seem to suggest sinless perfection in this life. But the intent of the words "commit sin" and similar phrases in 1 John is that of engaging in continual, habitual sinning. The word "practice" would be a clearer version of the word translated "commit." Read various versions to see how this truth is brought out. Also, note in verse 6a that the continuous aspect of abiding throws light on the continuous aspect of the verb "sinneth." (See Notes for more on this.)

Record below what this paragraph teaches about the following aspects of sin:

a definition of sin:

_____

source of sin:

_____

atonement for sin:

_____

a sinless person:

_____

power over sin:

_____

a specific example of sin:

_____

What do you think is meant by "the law" of verse 4?

_____

_____

What is referred to in the statement "the devil sinneth from the beginning" (3:8)?

_____

_____

3. *Paragraph 3:11-18*
Recall that this is the paragraph about love of the brethren. The paragraph teaches various bases or reasons for such love among Christians. List these, whether implied or explicitly stated, for each verse cited below:
3:11

_____

3:12-13

3:14

3:15

3:16

3:17

3:18

Why is hate classified as a sin of murder (3:15)?

What is meant by the statement "We ought to lay down our lives for the brethren" (v. 16)?

How can the good deed cited in the next verse (v. 17) fulfill the spirit of laying down one's life for a Christian brother?

4. *Paragraph 3:19-24*
What are the various words for *assurance* in these verses?

Why is assurance so important for healthy Christian living?

What does this paragraph teach about:
confidence in heart:

confidence in prayer:

confidence in abiding:

According to verse 22, answers to prayer are conditional upon what?

What are the two commandments of verse 23? Compare these with Jesus' conversation with a lawyer as recorded in Matt. 22:34-40.

According to verse 24, what are two evidences of the truth of Christ indwelling one's heart?

III. NOTES

1. "Doth not commit sin . . . cannot sin" (3:9). These are not references to sinless perfection in this life. (1 John 1:8–2:2 and other Scriptures do not support such a doctrine.) Rather, they refer to the habitual, unrepentant practice of sin, as indicated by the present tense of the Greek text. Concerning this tense, Wuest writes,

> "Commit" is **poieo** in the present tense which always speaks of continuous action unless the context limits it to punctiliar action, namely, the mere mention of the fact of the action, without the mentioning of details . . . "His seed" refers to the principle of divine life in the believer. It is this principle of divine life that makes it impossible for a Christian to live habitually in sin, for the divine nature causes the child of God to hate sin and love

righteousness, and gives him both the desire and the power to do God's will. . . .[1]

2. "The law" (3:4). Charles Ryrie writes, "Law is used in its broadest concept here and includes natural law (Rom. 2:14), the Mosaic law, the law of Christ (Rom. 8:2; 1 Cor. 9:21)."[2]

3. "Children of the devil" (3:10). Vincent quotes St. Augustine as saying, "The devil made no one, he begat no one, he created no one; but whosoever imitates the devil, is, as it were, a child of the devil, through imitating, not through being born of him."[3]

4. "God is greater than our heart" (3:20). The question of interpretation raised here is whether this superior greatness of God is related to His *judgment* or to His *compassion*. Of this, Vincent writes:

> If to His **judgment**, the sense is: God who is greater than our heart and knows all things, must not only **endorse** but **emphasize** our self-accusation. If **our heart** condemn, how much more **God**, who is greater than our heart. If to His **compassion**, the sense is: when our heart condemns us we shall quiet it with the assurance that we are in the hands of a God who is greater than our heart—who surpasses man in love and compassion no less than in knowledge. This latter sense better suits the whole drift of the discussion.[4]

IV. FURTHER ADVANCED STUDY

Two subjects appearing in this passage that may be studied in detail are: the devil (Satan) and God's law in this New Testament era. Recommended reading on the latter subject is Alva J. McClain, *Law and Grace*.

V. APPLICATIONS

Apply the truths of this passage to everyday living in these areas:
1. the Christian's hope
2. the Christian's righteous walk
3. love among Christians
4. the Christian's assurances

1. Kenneth S. Wuest, *In These Last Days*, pp. 140-50.
2. Charles C. Ryrie, "I, II, III John," in *The Wycliffe Bible Commentary*, p. 1473.
3. Quoted by A. T. Robertson in *Word Studies in the New Testament*, 2:348.
4. Ibid., p. 353

VI. WORDS TO PONDER

See what a wealth of love the Father has lavished on us, that we should be called God's children (3:1, *Berkeley*).

Lesson 8

Truth and Love

Chapter 4 is about two main subjects: truth in doctrine (vv. 1-6) and love in action (vv. 7-21). John had briefly mentioned this relationship between truth and love in 3:18: "Love . . . in truth." Now he dwells on the subject in detail. True doctrine is the foundation of life with God; Christian love is the natural expression of life with God. Let us study this passage to see how John develops this theme.

I. PREPARATION FOR STUDY

1. Read the following verses of John's three epistles where the word "truth" appears: 1 John 1:6, 8; 2:4, 21, 27; 3:18, 19; 4:6; 5:6; 2 John 1, 2, 3, 4; 3 John 1, 3, 4, 8, 12. Observe which verses refer to true *doctrine*.

2. Review your study of chapter 3, recalling how much John has written there about love. This is a good introduction to 4:7-21, which develops the subject thoroughly.

3. Review 2:18-23, recalling what these verses teach about antichrists. Were antichrists actual persons living in John's time?

4. Mark paragraph divisions in your Bible according to the references given below. Also mark in your Bible a main division at verse 7, dividing the chapter into two parts: Truth (4:1-6); and Love (4:7-21).

II. ANALYSIS

Segment to be analyzed: 4:1-21
Paragraph divisions: at verses 1, 7, 13, 17
Proceed with your analysis of this chapter, using methods of study suggested in the preceding lessons. Include these:

(1) marking the text of your Bible as you read
(2) key words and phrases
(3) main point of each paragraph
(4) main theme of 4:1-6; main theme of 4:7-21
(5) recording other observations and impressions on paper
(6) looking for intended contemporary applications of the Bible truths

Here are suggestions for studying the paragraphs individually:

A. Truth in Doctrine (4:1-6)

1. Note the references to spirit(s) and Spirit. (Observe how the last phrase of chap. 3 leads into the subject of this paragraph.) John refers to spirits here as though they were beings with audible voices (e.g., "Every spirit that confesseth not that Jesus Christ is come in the flesh..." (4:3). To whom is he really referring by this term? (Consider 4:1*b*, 3; 2:18-19, 22-23 in answering this.)

_____

_____

2. The false prophets of 4:1 are false teachers (cf. 2 Pet. 2:1). Recall from your study of Lesson 2 that one of the purposes of John in writing this epistle was to expose and condemn the false teaching of those who denied the real humanity of Jesus. Explain 4:2-3 in light of this.

_____

_____

Why was it necessary for Jesus to be a true, perfect man?

_____

_____

_____

3. Note the occurrences of the strong phrase "of God" in this paragraph. What is the meaning in each case?

_____

_____

_____

Extend this study to the remainder of the chapter.

_____

_____

4. What is the strength of the word "confesseth" in verse 2?

_____

_____

Is a person who merely assents to the factuality of Jesus' incarnation a child of God?
5. Who is meant by "them" in verse 4?

_____

_____

Explain "Greater is he that is in you, than he that is in the world" (4:4).

_____

_____

6. By way of summary, list below what this paragraph teaches about the spirit of truth and the spirit of error.

the spirit of truth	the spirit of error

B. Love in Action (4:7-21)

These remaining verses of chapter 4 teach many truths related to the subject of love. Read the passage and record below what is taught for each of the areas listed.

God's love for man

> love is of God (4:7)
> God sent His only begotten Son into the world
> He loved us —

Man's love for God

> not that we loved God

Christians' love for one another

> Let us love one another (4:7
> we ought also to love one another —

Who God is

> God is love (4:8)

What God has done

A Christian's relations to God

> everyone born of God - loves (4:7)
> He that loveth not - knoweth no (4:8)

1. *Paragraph 4:7-12*
What does John mean by the phrase of verse 8*a*, leading him to give the reason "for God is love"?

_____

_____

What truth about love is emphasized in verses 9 and 10?

_____

_____

What is the relationship between these phrases: "that we might live though him" (v. 9) and "the propitiation for our sins" (v. 10)?

_____

_____

Why did John include the sentence of verse 12*a* here? ("No man hath seen God at any time.")

_____

_____

2. *Paragraph 4:13-16*
Observe the repeated word "dwell" in this paragraph. Note that it is introduced by verse 12. What is meant by each of the two phrases:
"we dwell in him"

_____

"he in us"

_____

What is taught about Jesus in this paragraph?

_____

_____

Relate the doctrine of Christ's deity here (4:14-15) to that of His humanity, taught in 4:2. Why did the true man Jesus also have to be true God, in order to be the Saviour of the world?

_____

_____

3. *Paragraph 4:17-21*

Observe the repeated word "perfect" in this paragraph. The word "perfected" of verse 12 is related to this word. What does John seem to mean by a perfected love?

_____

What kind of fear is John referring to in verse 18? Compare this with the desirable fear spoken of by Peter in 1 Peter 1:17; 2:17.

_____

_____

III. NOTES

1. "Believe not every spirit" (4:1). The literal rendering is "Stop believing every spirit." It appears from this that some of John's readers had begun to accept some of the false Gnostic teachings that were circulating among the churches at that time.

2. "Try the spirits" (4:1). The word translated "try" in the King James is correctly represented in the *Berkeley Version* as "put to the test." The reference to spirits is to human beings—for example, teachers, pastors, evangelists—actuated either by demons (thus false) or the Holy Spirit (thus true).[1] (Cf. 1 Tim. 4:1).

3. "Confesseth that Jesus Christ is come in the flesh" (4:2). Of this *The Wycliffe Bible Commentary* says:

> He must openly acknowledge . . . the person of the incarnate Saviour. This involves the mode of his coming (**in the flesh**) and permanence of the incarnation (perfect tense of **come**). If he had not taken upon himself a human body, he could never have died and been the Saviour. From this verse we are not to suppose that this is the only test of orthodoxy, but it is a major one and it was the most necessary one for the errors of John's day.[2]

4. "God is love" (4:8). That is, "God as to His nature is love." John is the author of other short affirmations of God, such as "God is light" (1:5) and "God is a Spirit" (John 4:24). Vincent says, *"Spirit* and *light* are expressions of His *personality* corresponding to His nature."[3]

---

1. Kenneth S. Wuest, *In These Last Days*, p. 159.
2. Charles C. Ryrie, "I, II, III John," *The Wycliffe Bible Commentary*, pp. 1474-75.
3. Marvin R. Vincent, *Word Studies in the New Testament*, 2:357.

5. "His love is perfected in us" (4:12). The phrase "his love" refers to one of these: (1) God's love for us, (2) our love for God, (3) God's nature. Ryrie says, "It is probably not his love for us. If it is our love for him, this is *perfected* (matured) as we love the brethren. If it is the love which is his nature, that is *perfected* (or accomplishes its full purpose) as believers love one another."[4]

6. "We love him, because he first loved us" (4:19). The word "him" does not appear in the best Greek texts and so does not appear in many modern versions (e.g., *Berkeley, New American Standard*). Also, the verb "love" can be rendered as a subjunctive, with this reading: "Let us love, because He first loved us."

IV. FURTHER ADVANCED STUDY

Suggested topics for extended study are: the deity of Jesus; the humanity of Jesus; the world of evil spirits; main doctrines of modern liberal theology.

V. APPLICATIONS

1. Why is it important for Christians to critically evaluate new teachings as they appear on the contemporary scene under the label "Christian"?

2. What help does the Christian have in recognizing false doctrine ("spirit of error")?

3. Why is it important for a believer to be dwelling in God?

4. Cite at least three strong reasons for you as a Christian to love your brother in Christ.

5. Have you ever had an experience that proved the truth of this: "Perfect love casteth out fear" (4:18)?

VI. WORDS TO PONDER

It is the spirit of antichrist, of whose coming you have heard. Right now he is in the world (4:3; *Berkeley*).

4. Ryrie, p. 1475.

Lesson 9

Eternal Life

There can be no higher goal for a person than eternal life, for this is living with God forever. In an epistle that emphasizes fellowship with God, or living with God, one expects to find words and phrases that speak of this miraculous life from above. Such words are key words in chapter 5 of John's epistle, as we shall see in our study. The title of our lesson, "Eternal Life," is a favorite phrase of John's found fifteen times in his writings, including the passage of this lesson.[1] Our study of 5:1-12 will involve other subjects as well, but a main focus will be on the grand subject of eternal life.

I. PREPARATION FOR STUDY

1. Review the Survey Chart C, noting where the passage of this lesson fits into the pattern of 1 John.
2. Read the following verses on the terms shown, which represent John's usages of the terms in places of 1 John other than in the passage of this lesson. This will serve as a background to your study of this subject of eternal life.[2]

> "eternal life": 1:2; 2:25; 3:15; 5:13, 20
> "life": 1:1; 3:14; 5:16
> "born of God": 2:29; 3:9; 4:7; 5:18
> "children of God": 3:10; (4:4)
> "begotten of God": 5:18
> "sons of God": 3:1-2

---

1. John uses a similar phrase, "everlasting life," eight times (KJV), all references being in his gospel.
2. The phrase "of God" (e.g., "ye are of God"), which indirectly refers to this truth of divine life, is not listed here.

II. ANALYSIS

Segment to be analyzed: 5:1-12
Paragraph divisions: at verses 1, 4, 6, 9

A. General Analysis

1. Mark the paragraph divisions in your Bible, and proceed with the early stages of analysis as applied in earlier lessons.
2. Record the main theme of each paragraph:
5:1-3

_____

5:4-5

_____

5:6-8

_____

5:9-12

_____

3. Record key words and phrases:

_____

_____

4. What aspect of Christian life is referred to in the first two verses of the segment?

_____

_____

Compare this with the last two verses.

_____

_____

5. Observe every reference to "believe" in chapter 5.[3] What fruits of *believing* are cited in this segment?

_____

_____

3. The word "believe" appears only three times in this epistle prior to this chapter.

6. Complete this outline:

ETERNAL LIFE

Paragraph 1—Received by

_____

Paragraph 2—Given for

_____

Paragraph 3—Possible through

_____

Paragraph 4—Based on

_____

(See Chart J for one way to complete the outline.)
7. The phrase "of God" appears often throughout the passage. Make a topical study of this interesting subject.

B. Paragraph Analysis

Now study each paragraph by itself, where the units are sentences, phrases, and words.
1. *Paragraph 5:1-3*
In what ways does John identify a child of God in this paragraph? Compare your answer with 3:23.

_____

_____

The word "Christ" comes from the Greek root *krino*, meaning "to anoint." What is involved in a genuine, personal belief that Jesus is the "anointed one"?

_____

_____

What does this paragraph teach about love? (Note: Read v. 3a as, "For this is the love of God.")

_____

_____

_____

_____

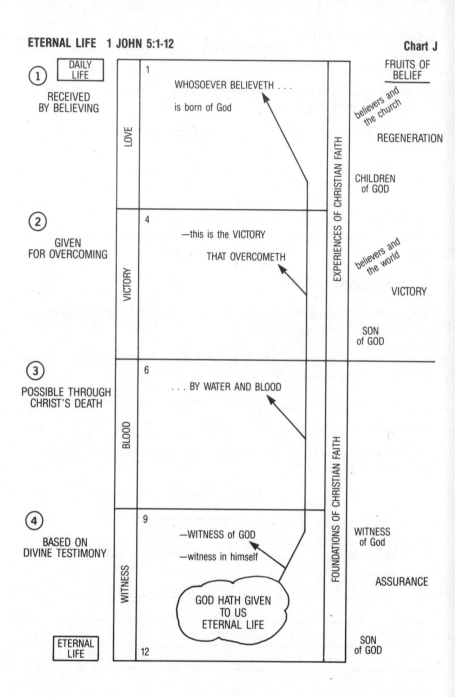

①

RECEIVED
BY BELIEVING

DAILY LIFE

1

WHOSOEVER BELIEVETH . . .

is born of God

LOVE

FRUITS OF BELIEF

believers and the church

REGENERATION

CHILDREN of GOD

②

GIVEN
FOR OVERCOMING

4

—this is the VICTORY

THAT OVERCOMETH

VICTORY

EXPERIENCES OF CHRISTIAN FAITH

believers and the world

VICTORY

SON of GOD

③

POSSIBLE THROUGH
CHRIST'S DEATH

6

. . . BY WATER AND BLOOD

BLOOD

FOUNDATIONS OF CHRISTIAN FAITH

④

BASED ON
DIVINE TESTIMONY

9

—WITNESS of GOD

—witness in himself

GOD HATH GIVEN
TO US
ETERNAL LIFE

WITNESS

ETERNAL LIFE

12

WITNESS of God

ASSURANCE

SON of GOD

2. *Paragraph 5:4-5*
What is meant by "the world" in these verses?

_____

_____

What situation involving the believer is implied by the word "overcometh"?

_____

Account for the different aspects of belief in these pairs: He who believes that Jesus is the Christ ⟶ is born of God (5:1).
He who believes that Jesus is the Son of God ⟶ overcomes the world (5:5).

_____

_____

3. *Paragraph 5:6-8*
Read these verses in different modern versions. See Notes on the spurious parts of verses 7 and 8. Also, see Notes on the phrase "water and blood."
What fact of Jesus' life is symbolized by blood?

_____

_____

Why the emphasis of blood in verse 6?

_____

What is the importance of the Spirit's witness concerning Jesus' ministry for man?

_____

What is John emphasizing by his reference to agreement in verse 8?

_____

_____

4. *Paragraph 5:9-12*
What witnesses are compared here?

_____

_____

What human witnesses may John have had in mind? Apply verse 9 to the contemporary scene.

_____

_____

Of what value is it for a Christian to have "the witness in himself" (v. 10)?

_____

_____

What is the prominent word of verses 11 and 12?

_____

_____

What various truths are taught in these verses?

_____

_____

How is this paragraph about witness led up to by what John writes in verses 6-8?

_____

_____

III. NOTES

1. *"His commandments are not grievous"* (5:3). The word translated "grievous" means literally "heavy."

2. *"Overcometh"* (5:4-5). The word appears three times in these two verses. The present tense is used in the first and last instances; the aorist tense, emphasizing a completed action, is used in the second instance. Hence the *Berkeley Version*'s rendering of these verses, shown at the end of this lesson under Word to Ponder.

3. *"The world"* (5:4). "Here the forces of the world-system of evil, the flesh (totally depraved nature), the devil, and the pernicious age-system . . . with which the saint is surrounded, are all engaged in a battle against the saint, carrying on an incessant war-

fare, the purpose of which is to ruin his Christian life and testimony."[4]

4. *"By water and blood"* (5:6). *The Wycliffe Bible Commentary* lists four interpretations that have been made of this couplet: (1) two events of Jesus' life: baptism and death; (2) the water and blood that flowed from Christ's side on the cross; (3) Christ's ministries of purification and redemption; (4) the church's sacraments of baptism and the Lord's Supper. The first view is the preferred one.[5] The Holy Spirit's agreement with these witnesses (5:8) concerns His present continuing work in this age. (Read the rendering of 5:6-8 in *The Living Bible*.)

5. *Verses 7 and 8*. The section from "in heaven" to "in earth" is considered spurious by most Bible scholars. One argument against its inclusion, cited by Ryrie, is that not a single manuscript earlier than the fourteenth century contains this trinitarian section.[6] Of course, the fact and doctrine of the Trinity are true. It is just that the doctrine does not depend on this spurious addition.

IV. FURTHER ADVANCED STUDY

Three different kinds of advanced study are suggested for this lesson:

1. Word studies: "believe"; and "witness."

2. Interpretation: Refer to various commentaries for interpretations of the phrase "water and blood."

3. New Testament text: Compare the readings of 5:7-8 in various versions, and consult outside sources for reasons for and against the inclusion of the trinitarian section here.

V. APPLICATIONS

1. In what sense are you, as a Christian, in conflict with "the world"? How can you be the victor from day to day?

2. What are some of the Holy Spirit's ministries to you now?

3. Can you think of any subtle or deceitful ways in which men, including theologians, are hiding the truth of God's Word from people these days?

4. On what are you basing your hope of life after death?

4. Kenneth S. Wuest, *In These Last Days*, p. 174.
5. Refer to Charles C. Ryrie, "I, II, III John," in *The Wycliffe Bible Commentary*, pp. 1476-77, for the reasons for preferring the first view.
6. Ibid., p. 1477

VI. WORD TO PONDER

Everyone who has been born of God conquers the world, and this is the victory that has triumphed over the world—the faith we have. Who is the world's victor, if not he who believes that Jesus is the Son of God? (5:4-5, *Berkeley*).

Lesson 10

Assurance of Eternal Life

John's inspiring epistle could not end on a higher, more climactic note than that of assurance and security. The last segment of nine verses is bathed in this atmosphere, with the words "we know" resounding over and over again in a symphony of triumph.

We are living in a world where people are groping in spiritual darkness, searching for answers. They want to know where they came from, why they are here, and where they are going. Their gravest concern involves their destiny after death. The gospels (lit. "glad tidings") were so named because they furnished all the answers to man's fundamental spiritual questions. This is what John had in mind as he was inspired to write *his* version of the gospel. In writing his epistle he wanted to show that those who believe and obey the gospel can and do know with assurance that the prize of eternal life, with all of its attendant blessings, is their own present and abiding possession.

I. PREPARATION FOR STUDY

1. Before reading the Bible text, ponder what it means to you to have assurance of eternal life. Remind yourself of what man does, on a mundane level, to attain limited "security" concerning such things as retirement income, death in the family, catastrophic accidents, and fires. What really is *security*, and on what does it basically depend?

2. Review your study made in Lesson 2 of the word *know* in 1 John.

II. ANALYSIS

Segment to be analyzed: 5:13-21
Paragraph divisions: at verses 13, 14, 18

A. General Analysis

1. First, a word might be said about the reasons for the paragraph divisions shown above. Read each of the three paragraphs and check your own conclusions with these:

First paragraph (5:13). This is just one verse. It seems to stand alone, serving in two capacities: (1) as a concluding statement for the entire epistle; (2) as an introductory statement for this last segment.

Second paragraph (5:14-17). Verses 14 and 15 are clearly about petitions in prayer (key word: "ask"). Verses 16 and 17 are included in this paragraph because they cite one *example* of a prayer request (see the words "ask" and "pray").

Third paragraph (5:18-21). Some versions justifiably print each verse as a different paragraph. But there is no reason for not bringing them together because of the binding phrase "we know." We will see in our study how verse 21 is tied in with verse 20.

2. Read the segment again carefully, noting key words and phrases. What appears to be a problem passage?

3. Underline in your Bible (if you have not already done this for Lesson 8) all references to spiritual life.

4. Underline the word *know* and words related to it as they appear in the text.

B. Paragraph Analysis

Now study the segment paragraph by paragraph.

1. *Paragraph 5:13*

Read this verse in various versions. You will find in most cases that the phrase "believe on the name of the Son of God" is not duplicated. This is based on the absence of the last phrase ("and that ye may believe on the name of the Son of God") from the best Greek manuscripts. What are your observations concerning these parts of the verse:

(1) "Believe on the name." Is more than mental assent meant here?

(2) "Son of God." Note other references to the Son in this segment.

(3) "That ye may know." Is this only mental knowledge?

2. Paragraph 5:14-17
What do verses 14 and 15 teach about confidence?

_____

_____

Note carefully the progressing sequence suggested by these verses:
    (1) "Ask according to God's will (14*a*).
    (2) He hears us (14*b*).
    (3) We have confidence that He hears us (15*a*).
    (4) The requests we ask of Him are assured us (15*b*).
Think of a purely selfish petition and apply it to the above sequence. Where does it fail?

_____

The passage of 5:16-17 is admitted by all to be a difficult one to interpret. In your study of the passage, move from the obvious to the unclear. Refer to outside helps for whatever assistance they may offer. The petition cited in verse 16 is prayer for whom by whom?

_____

Justify your answer.

_____

What kind of petitions should Christians bring to God concerning non-Christians?

_____

The words "death" and "life" refer here to either that which is physical or that which is spiritual. What do you think? Justify your answer.
Read the word "unto" as having the idea of "with a tendency to."[1]
Read "he shall give him life" as "He [God] shall give him life." (This is *God's* answer to the Christian's prayer. This does not negate the *Christian's* part in restoring a fellow believer to God, as taught by James 5:19-20. Read these verses.)

1. See Kenneth S. Wuest, *In These Last Days*, p. 182.

Does John make any reference to a Christian's sinning "a sin unto death"? Would John have held that antichrists were among those guilty of such sin?

What is the intent of the last sentence of verse 16?

Why do you think John inserts such an obvious truth as that of 17a in this context?

Read the following expanded paraphrase and commentary for its suggestions of possible interpretations of verses 16 and 17:

> If a Christian sees another Christian sin (not the kind of sin, such as rejection of Christ by unbelievers, which brings spiritual death), he shall petition God, who will restore life (that life of fellowship which was temporarily suspended by sin), which He does for Christians (who are not of those condemned to death for rejection of Christ). I am not speaking here about praying for those who deny Jesus Christ, which is a fatal sin. That is another matter (of which I have written much in my gospel). And to you who question why I am distinguishing between two types of sin, I say this: it is universally true that **all** unrighteousness is sin; but the sin of unbelief and rejection of Christ means spiritual death which is separation from God, whereas a sin committed by a child of God incurs not spiritual death but the temporary suspension of fellowship with God.

3. Paragraph 5:18-21
Observe the appearance of the phrase "we know" in these verses. Is there a logical progression involved in the listing?

Verse 18: Does this summarize a prominent doctrine of 1 John? How is the verse related to verse 17?

86

Verse 19: What contrast is made in the verse?

_____

_____

Verse 20: What is meant by "that we may know him"? Who is the "him"?

_____

_____

How does the Son give an "understanding" of "him"?

_____

_____

Verse 21: Observe the repetition of the word "true" in verse 20. How does this introduce the main point of verse 21, since idols are *false* gods?

_____

_____

What are your reflections as to how John has chosen to conclude his epistle?

_____

_____

III. NOTES

1. "He shall give him life" (5:16). The more natural interpretation reads "he" as referring to God. On the phrase "give him life," B.F. Westcott writes, "The sinner [the Christian sinning] is not 'dead,' nor yet 'sinning unto death,' but his life is, as it were, suspended in part. Comp. John x. 10."[2]

2. "Sin unto death" (5:16). Some interpret this as physical death.[3] Wuest prefers the view that this sin is "the denial of the incarnation, and that it is committed by an unsaved person who professes to be a Christian."[4]

---

2. B.F. Westcott, *The Epistles of St. John*, p. 192.
3. See H.A. Ironside, *Addresses on the Epistles of John*, pp. 216ff., for this view. *The Wycliffe Bible Commentary* says that this phrase refers to cases similar to those cited in 1 Corinthians 5 and 11:30 (p. 1477.)
4. Wuest, p. 182.

87

IV. FURTHER ADVANCED STUDY

You will find it a very interesting study to read how various commentators interpret 5:16-17. Most commentators admit frankly that this is a difficult passage to interpret fully.

V. APPLICATIONS

1. Are you experiencing a deep-seated assurance of possessing eternal life?
2. Do you bring petitions to God in true and strong faith?
3. Do you intercede for fellow Christians when you are aware that they have sinned (possibly even against *you*)?

VI. SUMMARY OF 1 JOHN

Before leaving your study of 1 John as you move into the next lessons, think back over this wonderful epistle and recall as many of its prominent teachings as you can. Write down a list of these.

VII. WORD TO PONDER

Little children, keep yourselves from idols (5:21).

From the thought of 'Him that is true' [5:20] St. John turns almost of necessity to the thought of the vain shadows which usurp His place. In them the world asserted its power. They forced themselves into notice on every side in innumerable shapes, and tempted believers to fall away from the perfect simplicity of faith. One sharp warning therefore closes the Epistle of which the main scope has been to deepen the fellowship of man with God and through God with man.[5]

5. Westcott, p. 197.

Lesson 11
John's Second Epistle

The second and third epistles of John have been called 'Twin sisters' because of similar length, style, and content. The best introduction to these epistles is a study of John's first letter, which we have just completed. Let us proceed with our study of 2 John with the advantage of this momentum.

I. BACKGROUND

A. Author

The writer identifies himself only as "the elder." Internal evidence and tradition point to the apostle John as the author.

B. Addressee

The epistle was written to "the elect lady and her children." This designation has two possible interpretations:
1. Figurative. By this the "elect lady" refers to a local church or the church as a whole; and "her children" refers to members of the church.
2. Literal. By this "the elect lady" is an unnamed lady; or her name is Cyria (Greek *eklekta kuria*, translated "elect Cyria"), or Electa (translating the Greek as "the lady Electa"). The lady was a Christian friend of John, mother of children, well known in her community, whose sister's children were probably residents of Ephesus.
    The informal, personal study of the epistle favors the literal view.

2 JOHN: TRUTH AND THE CHRISTIAN — "to the chosen lady"

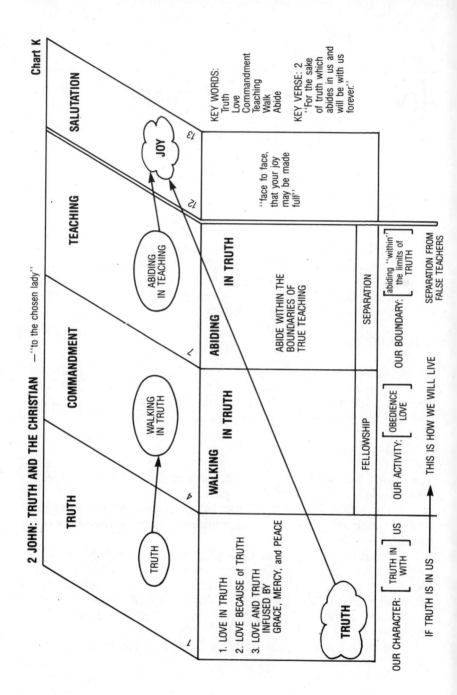

TRUTH	COMMANDMENT	TEACHING	SALUTATION

TRUTH

WALKING IN TRUTH

ABIDING IN TEACHING

JOY

1   4   7   12   13

TRUTH IN TRUTH	WALKING IN TRUTH	ABIDING IN TRUTH	

1. LOVE IN TRUTH
2. LOVE BECAUSE of TRUTH
3. LOVE AND TRUTH INFUSED BY GRACE, MERCY, and PEACE

ABIDE WITHIN THE BOUNDARIES OF TRUE TEACHING

"face to face, that your joy may be made full"

| | FELLOWSHIP | SEPARATION | |

| OUR CHARACTER: [TRUTH IN / WITH] US | OUR ACTIVITY: [OBEDIENCE / LOVE] | OUR BOUNDARY: [abiding "within" the limits of TRUTH] | |

IF TRUTH IS IN US → THIS IS HOW WE WILL LIVE

SEPARATION FROM FALSE TEACHERS

KEY WORDS:
Truth
Love
Commandment
Teaching
Walk
Abide

KEY VERSE: 2
"For the sake of truth which abides in us and will be with us forever."

C. Date and Place

Written around A.D. 90 from the city of Ephesus.

D. Canonicity

The second and third epistles of John were not recognized by the church as Holy Scripture as quickly as John's other writings. This is mainly explained by the fact that the letters took longer in becoming part of the churches' public reading programs because of their brevity and their appearance as merely private letters.[1] But the internal and external evidence is strong in favoring canonicity of these letters.

E. Occasion and Purpose

These will be observed in the studies that follow.

II. SURVEY

Read this short letter a few times, observing key words and phrases. Mark your Bible as you read.
What were some of the conditions existing at this time that occasioned the writing of the epistle?

_____

_____

What were some of John's main purposes in writing the letter?

_____

_____

The survey chart, Chart K, shows some of the highlights of 2 John, as well as related items. After you have read the epistle a few times, look over the survey chart. Refer back to it after you have _analyzed_ the epistle, when the chart will be even more meaningful.

III. ANALYSIS

Segment to be analyzed: the entire chapter (vv. 1-13)
Paragraph divisions: at verses 1, 4, 7, 12

---

1. These are the two shortest books of the Bible, 3 John being one line shorter than 2 John in the Greek text.

1. *Paragraph 1-3*

Observe the different ways in which John refers to truth. Is John intending a distinction by the two different terms "truth" and "the truth"? If so, what?

_____

_____

Write out a list of propositions based on these references.

_____

_____

_____

_____

Benedictions are used regularly in Christian church services, and so we have the tendency to overlook them because of their familiarity. Study carefully the benediction of verse 3. (See Notes on the grammatical construction of the verse.) Reflect on all the meanings attached to the three strong words "grace," "mercy, "peace." How does verse 3 teach the deity of Christ and the fact of *distinct* Persons within the Trinity?

_____

_____

2. *Paragraph 4-6*

What is the key repeated word of this paragraph? What various truths are taught about this subject?

_____

_____

What is taught here about (1) truth, (2) love, and (3) the Christian's walk?

_____

_____

_____

3. *Paragraph 7-11*

What does this paragraph teach about false doctrine and true doctrine?

_____

_____

Does the phrase "abideth in the doctrine of Christ" suggest that Christians should live within the boundaries of the doctrine of Christ? How does this harmonize with the freedom in Christ taught by Galatians 5:1?

_____

_____

Verse 10 is probably a reference to false teachers (such as the Gnostics who denied the humanity of Christ, v. 7) who were trying to disseminate their false doctrine in the local church that met in the elect lady's house.[2] The question of hospitality is not the issue here. It is a situation of a threat against the very life of the Christian community. On this Henry Alford has remarked, "It would have been infinitely better for the Church now, if this command had been observed in all ages by her faithful sons."[3] What can be learned from verses 10 and 11 about the responsibility of the local church today concerning speakers who occupy its pulpit?

_____

_____

4. *Paragraph 12-13*
Reflect on the significance of the phrase "Speak face to face, that our joy may be full."

IV. NOTES

1. *"Grace be with you" (v. 3)*. The Greek reads literally, "There shall be with us grace, mercy, peace. . . ." The spirit of benediction is present in either reading.
2. *Verse 8*. There is better manuscript support for this reading: " . . . that ye lose not those things which we have wrought, but that ye receive a full reward."
3. *"Neither bid him God-speed" (v. 10)*. The *Berkeley Version* gives the literal rendering "nor extend him your greeting."

V. FURTHER ADVANCED STUDY

Topical studies on each of the three words, "grace," "mercy," and "peace," are recommended.

---

2. Cf. Col. 4:15 for a similar house meeting place.
3. Henry Alford, *The Greek Testament*, 4:521.

VI. APPLICATIONS

1. Is your Christian life accurately described by the phrase "walking in truth"?
2. Is one of your purposes in Bible study to learn better what God's commandments to you are?
3. Are you aware of the growing trend of false liberal teaching in the schools and churches of our land? What can Christians do to effectively combat this?

VII. WORDS TO PONDER

Whoever assumes leadership, and does not remain in the doctrine of Christ, does not have God (v. 9, *Berkeley*).

Lesson 12
John's Third Epistle

One valuable contribution of the second and third epistles is their picture of typical local churches. These churches were existing a half century after Christ's ascension. Problems in churches today are not unique to this age. Concerning John's third epistle, Charles Ryrie says, "This brief and very personal letter shatters the notion that the state of things was ideal, or nearly so, in the first century. Contrariwise, it reveals the problems of a vigorously growing faith."[1] When considering this, one begins to see something of God's purpose in including such short letters as 2 and 3 John in His holy Book.

As you study 3 John, keep before your mind the church of the twentieth century. Observe what the epistle teaches, interpret the meanings, and apply these to the contemporary scene. Of course the epistle cannot speak about many of the aspects of church life, because of its brevity. But it does single out important items, thereby fulfilling its intended purpose.

I. BACKGROUND

A. Author, Date, and Place

The author is John the apostle; date and place are essentially the same as for 2 John: A.D. 90; the city of Ephesus.

B. Addressee

Third John is addressed to a man—Gaius, whereas 2 John is addressed to a woman. There is no way to identify who this Gaius was. The name itself was one of the most commonly used names

---

1. Charles C. Ryrie, "I, II, II John," in *The Wycliffe Bible Commentary*, p. 1483.

of the Roman Empire. Men of the New Testament with this name are:

Gaius of Macedonia (Acts 19:29)
Gaius of Derbe (Acts 20:4)
Gaius of Corinth (Rom. 16:23)

Gaius whom Paul baptized, who may be the same as the third-mentioned Gaius (1 Cor. 1:14)

There is no reference in 3 John to Gaius as being an official in the church. We may regard him as an active lay member, a personal friend of John. His character will be studied later in the lesson.

C. Occasion

An immediate occasion for writing this letter was Diotrephes' rejection of messengers of the gospel whom John had sent to the church, of which Gaius and Diotrephes were members (3 John 9-10).

II. SURVEY

Follow the same procedures of survey study for this letter as you did for 2 John. Chart L is the survey chart for 3 John.

III. ANALYSIS

Segment to be analyzed: the entire chapter (vv. 1-14)
Paragraph divisions: at verses 1, 2, 5, 9, 11, 13

A. General Analysis

Before analyzing each paragraph individually, make these studies in the epistle as a whole:
1. Compare 2 and 3 John as to:
    (1) salutation and conclusion
    (2) similar repeated words and phrases
    (3) tone
    (4) church problems
    (5) what is taught about God and Christ (account for the small amount of theological teaching in 3 John)
2. What three men are mentioned by name in 3 John?

_____

_____

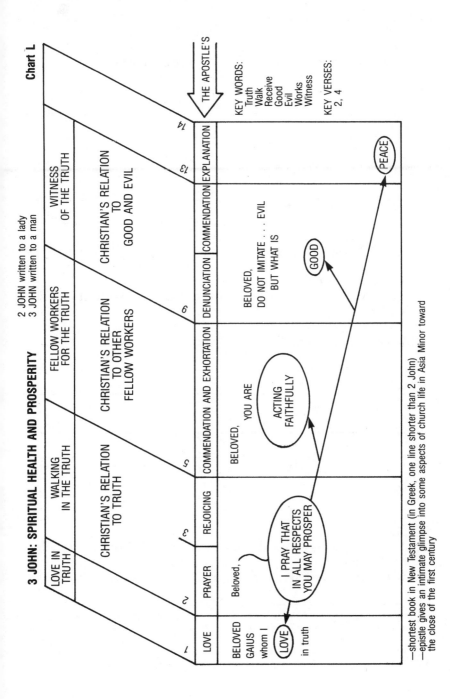

3 JOHN: SPIRITUAL HEALTH AND PROSPERITY

Chart L

2 JOHN written to a lady
3 JOHN written to a man

LOVE IN TRUTH	WALKING IN THE TRUTH	FELLOW WORKERS FOR THE TRUTH	WITNESS OF THE TRUTH
CHRISTIAN'S RELATION TO TRUTH		CHRISTIAN'S RELATION TO OTHER FELLOW WORKERS	CHRISTIAN'S RELATION TO GOOD AND EVIL

LOVE	PRAYER	REJOICING	COMMENDATION AND EXHORTATION	DENUNCIATION	COMMENDATION	EXPLANATION
1	2	3	5	9	13	14

BELOVED GAIUS whom I **LOVE** in truth

Beloved, **I PRAY THAT IN ALL RESPECTS YOU MAY PROSPER**

BELOVED, YOU ARE **ACTING FAITHFULLY**

BELOVED, DO NOT IMITATE . . . EVIL BUT WHAT IS **GOOD**

PEACE

← THE APOSTLE'S

KEY WORDS:
Truth
Walk
Receive
Good
Evil
Works
Witness

KEY VERSES:
2, 4

—shortest book in New Testament (in Greek, one line shorter than 2 John)
—epistle gives an intimate glimpse into some aspects of church life in Asia Minor toward the close of the first century

Make a character study of each, on the basis of what is written in the epistle.
3. What does this letter teach about Christian love?

_____

_____

_____

About truth?

_____

_____

_____

B. Paragraph Analysis

1. *Paragraph 1*
See how many spiritual lessons you can glean from this short salutation.
2. *Paragraph 2-4*
What is soul prosperity (v. 2)?

_____

_____

What brings this?

_____

_____

Explain the reason for John's greatest joy, expressed in verse 4.

_____

_____

3. *Paragraph 5-8*
Study this paragraph in the light of the last phrase, "fellow helpers to the truth."
What are the various teachings on hospitality in this paragraph?

_____

_____

_____

What is the significance of the additional phrase "and to strangers" (v. 5)?

_____

_____

Compare this with 2 John 10.
The phrase "for his name's sake" (v. 7) is correctly translated "for the sake of the name." Whose name is meant here? (Cf. Acts 5:41; James 2:7.)

_____

_____

4. *Paragraph 9-10*
What deep-seated evil heart attitude was Diotrephes guilty of?

_____

How is this a root of many kinds of sin?

_____

How are thoughts, deeds, and words mentioned in this paragraph?

_____

Observe the reference to "church" in this passage. John uses this word only in this epistle and in the book of Revelation.
5. *Paragraph 11-12*
What is the dominant contrast in this paragraph?

_____

6. *Paragraph 13-14*
What do these verses reveal about John?

_____

_____

_____

IV. NOTES

1. *"I wish above all things" (v. 2)*. A more accurate translation is "I pray that in all respects" (NASB*).
2. *"Bring forward on their journey" (v. 6)*. This refers to the supplying of necessary provisions for a person's journey. (Cf. Acts 15:3; Titus 3:13.)
3. *"Demetrius" (v. 12)*. There is no way of determining if this is the jeweler of Ephesus (Acts 19:23-27), now converted.

V. FURTHER ADVANCED STUDY

An extended study of Christian hospitality in the New Testament would be a profitable one.

VI. APPLICATIONS

Make a list of ten practical lessons for today taught by this epistle.

VII. A CONCLUDING NOTE ON JOHN'S EPISTLES

Greet the friends **by name** (v. 14).
He calleth his own sheep **by name** (Jn. 10:3).

John's epistles end on a bright, warm note in the last two words: "by name." The words are an appropriate reflection of the man who wrote them. A. Plummer writes, "S. John as shepherd of the Churches of Asia would imitate the Good Shepherd and know all his sheep by name."[2]

New American Standard Bible.
2. A. Plummer, *The Epistle of St. John*, p. 153.

Lesson 13
The Epistle of Jude

The epistle of Jude is a passionate plea to Christians to beware of spiritual contamination by evil men. Jude had originally intended to write a doctrinal epistle, dwelling on the grand subject of salvation. But the infiltration of false teachers and immoral persons into Christian circles had become so widespread that Jude was constrained by the Spirit to devote most of his letter to warning his fellow believers about this serious threat.

The Christian church today is not immune to the plagues that threatened the faith and fellowship of the first-century church. Let us as Christians learn from Jude's epistle all that we need to know to fortify our position and our program for the glory of God.

I. BACKGROUND

Let us first become acquainted with the setting of Jude's epistle, to the extent of that which is known or strongly inferred.

A. Author and Addressee

The author is identified in verse 1 by (1) name: Jude; (2) kinship: brother of James; and (3) relation to Christ: servant (bondslave). There are strong reasons for believing that this James was the half brother of Jesus, which associates Jude with Jesus in the same way. (On James, read Matt. 13:55; Mark 6:3; Acts 12:17; 15:13; 21:18ff.; Gal. 1:19; 2:9). If this is so, then Jude became a believer after Christ's resurrection (cf. John 7:5 and Acts 1:14). From verse 17 we gather that Jude did not class himself as an apostle.

Those to whom Jude wrote this letter may have been members of Jewish churches of Palestine or Asia Minor, where he probably was ministering at this time.

B. Date

A suggested date for the writing of the epistle is around A.D. 67-68, shortly before the fall of Jerusalem (A.D. 70).[1]

C. Occasion and Purpose

Jude clearly states in his epistle what impelled him to write what he did. The leaven of such evils as gross immorality, antinomianism, rejection of the lordship of Christ, and mockery, was beginning to spread in the churches through the influences of "certain men" (e.g., v. 4).[2] This stirred Jude to write what Dean Alford has called "an impassioned invective, in the impetuous whirlwind of which the writer is hurried along ... laboring for words and images strong enough to depict the polluted character of the licentious apostates against whom he is warning the Church."[3] It is for this content that S. Maxwell Coder calls the book of Jude "The Acts of the Apostates." Read verses 3, 17, 21, and 22 for Jude's commands to his readers in view of the threatening situation.

D. Canonicity

Like 2 and 3 John, Jude was not recognized as canonical as early as were the longer books of the New Testament. But it is clearly a part of Holy Writ.

II. SURVEY

The survey Chart M shows the structural parts and key subjects of Jude's epistle. Observe from the chart how orderly the book's pattern is. Refer to this chart as you work on the survey and analysis exercises given in the remainder of the lesson.

1. Read the epistle once or twice for initial observations.
2. What is the general tone of the epistle? What is Jude's main burden?

---

1. See Chart A. If vv. 17 and 18 refer to things Peter wrote in 2 Peter (e.g., 3:3), then Jude was written after Peter's epistles.
2. The word antinomianism comes from *anti-nomos* ("against law"), and represents a libertine spirit that rejects the restrictions of commandments as such.
3. Quoted by J.H. Kerri, *Introduction to the New Testament* (New York: Revell, 1931), p. 308.

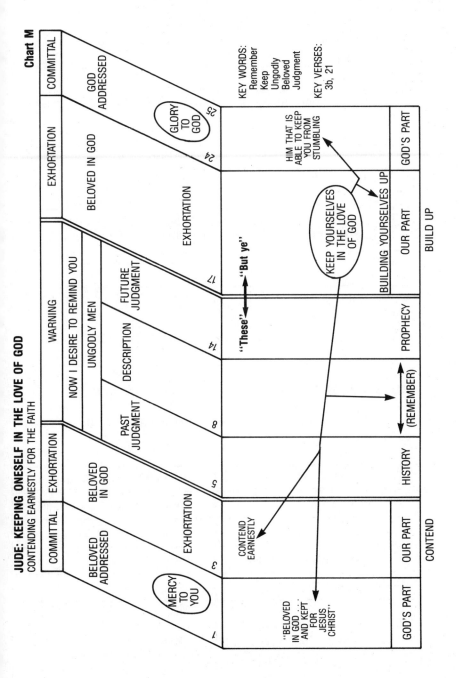

JUDE: KEEPING ONESELF IN THE LOVE OF GOD
CONTENDING EARNESTLY FOR THE FAITH

Chart M

COMMITTAL	EXHORTATION	WARNING	EXHORTATION	COMMITTAL

BELOVED ADDRESSED — BELOVED IN GOD — NOW I DESIRE TO REMIND YOU — BELOVED IN GOD — GOD ADDRESSED

EXHORTATION

UNGODLY MEN

PAST JUDGMENT — DESCRIPTION — FUTURE JUDGMENT

MERCY TO YOU

GLORY TO GOD

HIM THAT IS ABLE TO KEEP YOU FROM STUMBLING

KEEP YOURSELVES IN THE LOVE OF GOD

BUILDING YOURSELVES UP

"But ye"

"These"

(REMEMBER)

CONTEND EARNESTLY

"BELOVED IN GOD ... AND KEPT FOR JESUS CHRIST".

GOD'S PART	OUR PART	HISTORY	PROPHECY	OUR PART	GOD'S PART

CONTEND

BUILD UP

3 5 8 14 17 24 25 1

KEY WORDS:
Remember
Keep
Ungodly
Beloved
Judgment

KEY VERSES:
3b, 21

103

3. Compare the first two and the last two verses.

4. What are some of the key words and phrases of the letter?

5. Look for a main theme of each paragraph. Also, observe a key verse for the epistle.

6. Where is there a main turning point in the epistle?

7. Jude has been called the "vestibule to the book of Revelation." What future events are cited prophetically by Jude?

8. From the things Jude says, how intimately did he know his readers?

III. PREPARATION FOR ANALYSIS

For background to Jude's references to the past, read the passages cited below:

JUDE PASSAGE	EVENT REFERRED TO
v. 5 (Israelites)	Num. 13-14 (cf. 1 Cor. 10:5-10)
v. 6 (fallen angels)	cf. 2 Pet. 2:4 (see Notes)
v. 7 (Sodom and Gomorrah)	Gen. 18-19
v. 11 (Cain)	Gen. 4
v. 11 (Balaam)	Num. 22-24
v. 11 (Korah—"Core," KJV)	Num. 16
v. 14 (Enoch)	cf. Gen. 5:18-24 (see Notes)

IV. ANALYSIS

Segment to be analyzed: verses 1-25
Paragraph divisions: at verses 1, 3, 5, 8, 14, 17, 24
Study the epistle paragraph by paragraph, keeping in mind the survey Chart M and the main themes of each of the paragraphs.

A. Paragraph 1-2

1. How does Jude identify himself in verse 1? Compare the similar opening verse of James's letter. What does such a relationship to Christ involve?

_____

_____

2. What three verbs in verse 1 identify a believer's relation to the Father and the Son? (Note: Read the King James Version's "sanctified" as "loved," on the basis of the best Greek manuscripts.)

_____

_____

3. Reflect on all that is suggested by the combination of mercy, peace, and love, in verse 2. What is the strength of the phrase "be multiplied"?

_____

_____

4. What is emphasized in this opening paragraph: God's work or our work?

_____

_____

B. Paragraph 3-4

1. Compare this paragraph with the preceding one, as to what is emphasized: God's part or our part.

_____

_____

2. What is the key command of this paragraph? What is the strength of the words "earnestly" and "once delivered"? In what ways can a believer today put this command into obedient action?

_____

_____

3. How does verse 4 suggest what Jude means by the command of verse 3?

_____

4. What sins are identified in verse 4? Are these "certain men" true believers, professing believers, or unbelievers?

_____

_____

C. Paragraph 5-7

The clue to this paragraph is the first phrase, summed up in one word: _Remember._ Jude cites three historical situations to illustrate one universal, timeless truth. What is that truth? How is it related to what Jude has already said in his epistle?

_____

1. Reconcile the two phrases of verse 5: "having saved" and "afterward destroyed."

_____

2. How is an example of judgment on *angels* (v. 6) an example to *people*?

_____

3. How are these phrases consistent with the character of God: "everlasting chains . . . judgment of the great day" (v. 6) "vengeance of eternal fire" (v. 7)?

D. Paragraph 8-13

1. Who are the persons or beings cited in verse 9?

_____

What does each have to do with the illustration of *authority* given here?

_____

What truth about authority is taught in the verse? How does verse 8 lead into this? (Read vv. 9 and 10 in a modern paraphrase, such as *The Living Bible*, for clarification.)

_____

2. What sins does Jude expose in each of the following verses:
v. 8

_____

v. 10

_____

v. 11

_____

v. 12

_____

v. 13

_____

3. What *descriptions* of evil men are suggested by the metaphors of verses 12-13:
"spots" ("dirty spots," *Today's English Version*)

_____

"clouds"

_____

"trees"

_____

"waves"

_____

"stars"

E. Paragraph 14-16

1. What is the main teaching of verses 14-15?

2. How does verse 16 add to what Jude has already written in describing evil men?

F. Paragraph 17-23

Verse 17 marks a turning point in the epistle. The clue words to Jude's new subject are "But . . . ye." Compare this with the word "these" in the verses preceding this paragraph (vv. 8, 10, 12, 14, 16).
1. Concentrate your study on the commands found in the paragraph. Record the command verbs of these verses:
v. 17

v. 21

v. 22

v. 23

2. In connection with the command verbs noted above, there are various "ing" words, which qualify the commands. Record the "ing" words below, and indicate how they qualify each command:
v. 20

v. 20

v. 21

v. 22

_____

v. 23

_____

v. 23

_____

G. Paragraph 24-25

1. What do these concluding verses teach about God's work for the believer? Compare the phrases "keep you from" and "present you before."

_____

2. What words describe the believer in verse 24? What words describe God in verse 25?

_____

3. How are the last two *paragraphs* of this epistle Jude's solution to the problem he has described in verses 3-16? Is your heart moved to read such a doxology as this (vv. 24-25), written at the close of a practical letter about serious problems?

_____

4. What do you consider to be the most important teachings of Jude? Write these out in your own words.

_____

_____

_____

V. NOTES

1. *"Angels which kept not their first estate" (v. 6).* Peter also teaches the fact of the fall of evil angels (2 Pet. 2:4). Some identify Lucifer, who became Satan, as one of these angels, deriving their interpretation from Isaiah 14:12-17; Ezekiel 28:12-19; Revelation 12:4; and Matthew 25:41. Others hold that Jude 6 refers to Genesis

6:1-4.[4] Many Bible students believe that no Bible account records the details of this event.

2. *"Yet Michael the archangel" (v. 9).* Jude is probably citing a story given in the apocryphal book *Assumption of Moses.* In so doing, Jude is not recognizing the book as having canonical status, but he is recognizing the event as being factual. The same principle applies to his quote of the book of Enoch in verses 14-15.

3. *"Enoch . . . prophesied" (v. 14).* Of the apocryphal Book of Enoch, Wuest writes:

> This book, known to the Church Fathers of the second century, lost for some centuries with the exception of a few fragments, was found in its entirety in a copy of the Ethiopic Bible in 1773 by Bruce. It consists of revelations purporting to have been given to Enoch and Noah. Its object is to vindicate the ways of divine providence, to set forth the retribution reserved for sinners, and to show that the world is under the immediate government of God.[5]

Bible scholars are not in agreement as to whether Jude is here quoting from the apocryphal Book of Enoch or referring to an unrecorded prophecy of the Enoch of Genesis 5.[6]

4. *Verse 18.* The language of this verse and 2 Peter 3:3 is similar. *The Wycliffe Bible Commentary* says, "Both passages may look back to a current oral tradition of the teaching of the apostles."[7]

VI. FURTHER ADVANCED STUDY

1. Study the similarities of the epistles of Jude and 2 Peter. With the aid of outside sources, reach a conclusion as to how these similarities can be accounted for. (E.g., did Jude use Peter's letter as a source?)

---

4. See S. Maxwell Coder, *Jude, the Acts of the Apostates*, pp. 36-43, for a defense of this view.
5. Kenneth S. Wuest, *In These Last Days*, p. 251.
6. See Charles C. Ryrie, "I, II, III John," in *The Wycliffe Bible Commentary*, p.
7. Ibid.

2. Read what various authors have written concerning these subjects.[8]

(1) the Bible's full teaching about the evil angels' fall (v. 6)

(2) Jude's source for his reference to Michael the archangel (v. 9) and to Enoch (vv. 14-15)

VII. APPLICATIONS

What forces threaten Christ's church today, similar to those mentioned in the epistle?

In your own words, paraphrase Jude 17-25 as the verses apply to Christians today.

VIII. WORDS TO PONDER

Glory, majesty, might and authority, from all ages past, and now, and for ever and ever! Amen (v. 25).

What a way to end a letter! Before the stars were set in their courses to mark off time, throughout all the ages that have been recorded in heaven since time began, and on into the measureless future of God's unfolding purposes, these four divine attributes have belonged, do now belong, and will forever belong to God. In the wonder of the contemplation of such truths, THE PEN OF THE INSPIRED APOSTLE IS LAID DOWN, HIS LIPS BECOME DUMB.[9]

---

8. A highly recommended book for supplementary study is S. Maxwell Coder, *Jude, The Acts of the Apostates.*
9. Ibid., p. 127.

Bibliography

SELECTED SOURCES FOR FURTHER STUDY

Alford, Henry. *The Greek Testament.* Vol. 4. Chicago: Moody, 1958.

Burdick, Donald W. *The Letters of John the Apostle.* Chicago: Moody, 1970.

Candish, R. S. *The First Epistle of John.* Grand Rapids: Zondervan, 1952.

Coder, S. Maxwell. *Jude, the Acts of the Apostates.* Everyman's Bible Commentary. Chicago: Moody, 1958.

Drummond, R. J., and Morris, Leon. "The Epistles of John." In *The New Bible Commentary*, ed. F. Davidson. Grand Rapids: Eerdmans, 1953.

Gingrich, Raymond E. *An Outline and Analysis of the First Epistle of John.* Grand Rapids: Zondervan, 1943.

Hiebert, D. Edmond. *An Introduction to the Non-Pauline Epistles.* Chicago: Moody, 1962.

Ironside, H. A. *Addresses on the Epistles of John.* New York: Loizeaux, n.d.

Jensen, Irving L. *Jensen's Survey of the New Testament.* Chicago: Moody, 1981.

Leaney, A. R. C. *The Letters of Peter and Jude.* The Cambridge Bible Commentary. Cambridge: U. Press, 1967.

Manton, Thomas, *Exposition of the Epistles of Jude.* London: Nesbet, 1871.

Mayor, J. B. *Epistle of St. Jude and the Second Epistle of St. Peter.* London: Macmillan, 1907.

Moffatt, James. *The General Epistles: James, Peter, and Judas.* New York: Harper, n.d.

Plummer, A. *The Epistles of St. John.* Cambridge Greek Testament. Cambridge: U. Press, 1916.

Robertson, A. T. *Word Studies in the New Testament*. Vols. 2, 6. New York: Harper, 1933.

Robertson, Robert. "The General Epistle of Jude." In *The New Bible Commentary*, ed. F. Davidson. Grand Rapids: Eerdmans, 1953.

Ryrie, Charles C. "I, II, III John." In *The Wycliffe Bible Commentary*, ed. C. F. Pfeiffer and E. R. Harrison. Chicago: Moody, 1962.

Smith, David. "The Epistles of John." In *The Expositor's Greek Testament*. Vol. 5. Grand Rapids: Eerdmans, n.d.

Strong, James. *The Exhaustive Concordance of the Bible*. New York: Abingdon, 1890.

Thomas, W. H. Griffith. *Life and Writings of the Apostle John*. Grand Rapids: Eerdmans, 1946.

Unger, Merrill F. *Unger's Bible Handbook*. Chicago: Moody, 1966.

Vincent, Marvin R. *Word Studies in the New Testament*. Vol. 2. Grand Rapids: Eerdmans, 1946.

Vine, W. E. *An Expository Dictionary of New Testament Words*. Westwood, N.J.: Revell, 1940.

Wallace, David H. "The Epistle of Jude." In *The Wycliffe Bible Commentary*, ed. C. F. Pfeiffer and E. F. Harrison. Chicago: Moody, 1962.

Westcott, B. F. *The Epistles of St. John*. 3d ed. Grand Rapids: Eerdmans, 1950.

Williams, R. R. *The Letters of John and James*. The Cambridge Bible Commentary. Cambridge: U. Press, 1965.

Wuest, Kenneth S. *In These Last Days*. Grand Rapids: Eerdmans, 1954. References to eschatological subjects appearing in Jude.

Young, Robert. *Analytical Concordance to the Bible*. Grand Rapids: Eerdmans, n.d.